Advance P

"The book provides a pragmatic and inspiring road map to improve the effectiveness of teams in the modern-day organization that will create a people and business competitive advantage."
Ronan O'Loan, Former CHRO, F5 Networks

"Simon Mac Rory understands the dynamic of teams and organizations and provides an insightful and thought-provoking approach to the team-based organization of tomorrow."
Anne Heraty, CEO, Cpl Resources

"*Wake Up and Smell the Coffee* is an essential book for leaders and business people interested in creating a dynamic and authentic brand that stands apart and stands out from the competition."
Robin Hayes, CEO, JetBlue

"Simon Mac Rory brings fresh perspectives and a practical approach that drives teams' capacity to succeed. This book will help any business leader transform the way they approach teamwork to strengthen their organization and prepare it for the future."
Linda Jingfang Cai, Senior Director, Global Head of
Learning & Development, Aon

"Simon hits the nail on the head in addressing the reality of how critical teams are becoming in our ever-changing and inter-dependent world. Removing hierarchies and inventing more engaging and liberating workplaces for today's talent requires mindful design and this book will help both the sceptical and the converted"
Michael Pantlin, Executive Director of People,
Barts Health NHS Trust

Published by
LID Publishing Limited
The Record Hall, Studio 204,
16-16a Baldwins Gardens,
London EC1N 7RJ, UK

524 Broadway, 11th Floor, Suite 08-120,
New York, NY 10012, US

info@lidpublishing.com
www.lidpublishing.com

A member of:

BPR
Business Publishers Roundtable

www.businesspublishersroundtable.com

Printed in Great Britain by TJ International
ISBN: 978-1-911498-86-5

Cover design and layout: Matthew Renaudin

Wake up and smell the coffee

The imperative of teams

Simon Mac Rory

LONDON   NEW YORK   SHANGHAI
MADRID   BARCELONA   BOGOTA
MEXICO CITY   MONTERREY   BUENOS AIRES

Contents.

Acknowledgments.

This book is the product of many years working with teams across the globe. I often find in working with clients I learn as much if not more from them as they do from me. Much of the inspiration and content of this effort stem from the privilege granted to me by these teams and the open and engaged manner in which they worked with me. My thanks to all of them.

All of my colleagues at The ODD Company are contributors to this work and in particular I wish to express my gratitude to T.J. Byrne and Min Boruta, who have selflessly supported me and went well above and beyond the call of duty throughout this project.

The team at LID Publishing have made this journey so much more achievable in their support, advice and readiness to answer all my questions regardless of how mundane or frivolous. Their ongoing encouragement and availability made the challenge attainable and certainly checked the rising panic on occasion.

My sister Avril has proof read, opened up her contacts to me and supported me without question despite the outrageous assumptions I can make at times in the expectation of support of family – thanks, Sis.

And finally, my enduring thanks and love to my wife, Angelica, who as always is a rock in my life and encourages all that I do and even some of things that I shouldn't do!

Introduction.

For more than 20 years now I have had the privilege to work with teams across the world as a team coach and as a team facilitator. It has been exciting, engaging, rewarding and at times frustrating, but it has afforded me a fantastic insight into the dynamics of teams and the challenges that both teams and organizations face in delivering effective teamwork. *Wake Up and Smell the Coffee* as a title, in many ways, reflects that element of frustration I sometimes experience in working with clients. Teamwork is such a quintessential and critical element of organizational life and at times I wonder why some organizations just do not seem to grasp this concept. Teams are an imperative to agile and effective organizational performance. With a consistent and sustained effort much can be achieved in terms of improving team effectiveness and the associated benefits of increased productivity and impact to the bottom line.

Around 90% of what we do in the organization today happens through collaborative effort. This makes teamwork the imperative that it is. In today's challenging and increasingly complex business environment we need teams to deliver. If the organization can deliver a 5% improvement across the entire organization in terms of team effectiveness, imagine the impact to the bottom line. I believe that the approach I advocate, if implemented across the organization, can deliver up to a 20% improvement in effectiveness.

Throughout the nineties and noughties teams and teamwork were not high on the organizational agenda. In more recent times teams have risen to the top of the agenda again as organizations seek to meet the challenges of an increasingly complicated world. Agile responses, the rise of teams and the delivery of organizations as a network of teams have become a major focal point and challenge for organizations. Social media is providing a continuous stream of commentary in this arena, but I have not seen the expected action from organizations that is being suggested. I really do believe it is time for organizations to wake up and smell the coffee and address the issue of teams.

The term 'team' is an often poorly understood concept in the organization and the manner in which it is bandied about leads

to confusion and often misdirected expectations. I define a team
as a group of people, normally fewer than ten, that need to work
together to achieve a common goal, normally with a single leader
and where there is a high degree of interdependence between the
team members to achieve the goal or goals.

Unfortunately, we have a tendency to refer to departments and
entire functions as teams. Take HR as an example: in a large organization, there may be 50 to 100 people in the function, within which
there will be departments, within which there will be teams. When
I speak about a team I am talking about this subset of a department,
which, in turn, is a subset of the function. Hence the confusion with
the term in many instances. What starts out as a true team, in terms
of size, grows and expands into a department with multiple teams
and finally into a function with multiple departments, but we still
refer to it as 'the team'.

Teamwork is not rocket science and there are no magic formulas
or silver bullets. I firmly believe the vast majority of teams have it
within themselves to substantially improve their own effectiveness
without outside help. To do so they need to make time for reflection on 'how' they do things rather than on 'what' they do. They
need to do this in a structured way with a robust methodology that
is self-managing for the team and not reliant on experts being available. For this to have impact the organization must also contribute and must put in place a corporate team strategy that supports
all teams in the organization, delivering a common language and
model for teamwork that works for them. They need to link team
performance to both business metrics and individual performance.
They must grasp the difference between team types and recognize
that it is not a 'one size fits all' scenario. For example, the needs of a
virtual team are radically different to the needs of a traditional team
from inception through operation and delivery.

Delivering a team-based organization (a holy grail for many
today) is about culture and the 'way things are done around here'.
It is about a radical rethink on organizational structure. There is a
need to move away from the traditional hierarchy and this takes

time and investment. HR spend on technology has increased in dramatic terms. I suggest that while this is all very well and good, there needs to be an equal spend and focus on organizational structure and the delivery of truly team-based cultures if the power and the imperative of teams are to be delivered and the value of new technology realized.

This book is offered in three parts and is written for team members, team leaders and the organization.

Part 1 seeks to put the imperative of teams in context and examine why we must now address the issue of strategy for teams and structure for our organizations. It is a call to action.

Part 2 lays out the strengths, weaknesses, challenges and imperatives for the basic team types in play today.

Part 3 is a guide for team leaders and team members on how to drive team effectiveness for themselves. Twelve criteria for team effectiveness are explored and guidance provided for the team and the team leader in addressing them. Ignoring any one of these criteria can bring a team down, but no one on its own will make the team as effective as it can be.

All teams, no matter where they reside in the organization, can be better than they are today. All can improve. They need the strategy for teaming from the organization and they need the time to be reflective and address the issues outlined in this book.

In the spirit of the book's title, I have used coffee quips throughout, at the end of each chapter or critical section. I have included these quips as *aides-mémoire* and hope they will help the reader to recall and internalize some of the key points. I must admit, the research for the quips has resulted in me now knowing as much about coffee as I hope I do about teams!

So grab a cup of coffee, have a read and think about your team, your organization and what it is you need to do to finally realize the power of teams.

Part 1.

Smell the coffee

There are many factors and issues that impact the performance of teams. These are concerns for the team itself and for the organization overall. From the impact of generational changes to the very nature of employment, to the need to create more agile and responsive organizations, the team has become a critical element.

Part 1 is a call to action for organizations to address the issue of teamwork and recognize that teamwork and robust corporate team strategies are actual solutions to the many challenges we face today.

Over four chapters the imperative of teams are considered in the context of the gig economy, millennials and the rise of the team-based organization. Some of the more inaccurate perceptions of teams and teamwork are explored and the current topical concerns that are gripping attention are discussed. Throughout Part 1 there is a call for a more structured approach to team development and implementation, seeking the development of corporate team strategies and the deployment of team models to ensure consistency of approach in organizations.

It really is time to 'wake up and smell the coffee' when it comes to teams in our organizations. The organization that delivers for teams will deliver for its customers and gain that ever-important competitive advantage.

Chapter 1.

The imperative of teams

Imperative

Vital importance, crucial, essential, urgent.
Ninety per cent of what we do in organizations happens through
collaborative effort creating an imperative for effective teams.

Teamwork is the signature adaptation of our species according to David Sloan Wilson, an American evolutionary biologist.[1] Other species do it as well, but we are the masters. When one observes many work teams, one must question the veracity of this statement.

It is natural for us to collaborate and, in many aspects of our lives, we do it very well – one might think instinctively. Take the family unit or our social lives as an example. The family can be described as a team. For the most we (the team) are very effective in managing family life. Look closely at the family unit and you will quickly see the incredible planning, the evaluation, the communication, the clear goals, the established roles, the organization, the trust and so on. We plan for our children, we budget for the week, the month, we identify schools, child care and we make sure that there is food in the fridge, plan meals and we do not forget to pick up or arrange for the kids to be collected from school. We plan weekend activities, we go on holidays. All of this equates to some serious teamwork. In our social lives we do not walk out of the door on an evening, turn left or right on a whim and hope that we have a good night out. Oh, no – we plan the evening, often weeks in advance, we budget for it, we decide (goals) with friends, meet at a specific location and even have inbuilt evaluation methods to determine if it was a good night out and if we will do it again.

When we go to work, however, we seem to park these instinctive teaming skills outside the door. Often, it is the case that individuals and organizations seem to think that by simply putting together a group of people and calling them a 'team' they will perform as a team. There is even the belief that most teams are high performing. Actually, high-performing and effective teams are the exception rather than the rule. I would even go so far as to say that they are rare. There is no doubt in my mind that no matter the level of the team, including the CEO and their team, even the highest performing team can be better than they are today.

Organizations seem to think that teamwork happens by magic. If they did not, there would be evidence to the contrary. There would be a corporate team strategy. There would be a requirement for all teams to reflect on how they do things, not just what they do. There would be minimum standards for all teams. Team output would be linked to business metrics and individual performance. Teamwork would be integrated into organizational development, learning and development, and business strategies. Sadly, this is not the case.

For many years, teams and teamwork have not received the attention they deserve, to the detriment of the organization. They have not been on the agenda in any meaningful sense. I suggest that 90% of organizational output is achieved through teams. I base this on my experiences and observations of working with many organizations over many years. I seldom today find a truly individual contributor. The work of the organization is now so integrated it is almost impossible to find tasks that are not based on some form of collaborative effort. An organization with a defined strategy for teams, and the commitment to see it through, can drive a 10% to 20% improvement in effectiveness, productivity and impact to the bottom line.

Teams are back and relentlessly moving to the top of the agenda. For the past 20 years there has been little research on teams and the subject has not been a priority for most organizations. The individual agenda took over; talent management and 'star performers' was the mantra of the nineties and noughties.

However, there is new thinking about teams, and organizations who want to be competitive tomorrow need to take note today.

The power of teams

There is no question that, when properly deployed, teamwork is extremely powerful and drives many benefits for both the individual and the organization. This creates an imperative for organizations to take the issue of teamwork in a more serious and focused manner. Among the many benefits to be derived are:

Efficiency – The ability to focus different minds on the same problem leads to faster speed in problem resolution and delivery. The sum is always greater than the parts; teams can accomplish more than an individual and tend to create quality outcomes over and beyond the capacity of an individual working on their own.

Innovation and creativity – Teams are more creative and risk-oriented. They are more likely to think outside the box and generate novel and innovative solutions because of the support the team offers. An individual is more likely to adopt the safe option, the tried-and-tested approach. A team maximizes strengths and minimizes weaknesses.

Enhanced working environment – The mutual support a team can offer through shared goals drives achievement that an individual might not have the confidence to attempt on their own. The social aspect of a team provides a better work experience that can help foster motivation. The team environment increases accountability as individuals do not want to let the team down – 'peer pressure' if you will. The highs are better celebrated in a team and the lows better managed, whereas the lows for an individual can be paralysing and the highs for the individual, well, whom do they 'high-five'?

Minimize risk – Teams increase project momentum and mitigate the impact of sick leave, parental leave, vacations, etc. With an individual, a project comes to an abrupt halt in these situations. A team spreads the risk, has protocols and documentation that allows others on the team pick up a role and carry on. Teams have built-in flexibility.

Learning and talent – Teams deliver exponential learning compared to an individual working on their own. Shared perspectives, ideas and skills transfers, along with faster completion times on projects, see team members learn from each other and participate in more projects. The individual working on their own completes less projects, gets less experience and does not have the opportunity to challenge or be challenged in terms of their ideas. Effective teams attract talent. Who does not want to be a part of success?

These attributes are available to every team in every organization, but they do not happen by accident. They certainly do not happen just because you put a group of talented people together, call them a team and stand back. It takes hard work, it takes strategy, it takes an organization that enables teamwork. It requires a culture that recognizes the importance of teamwork – the imperative that it is today – and one where teaming is an inbuilt part of how things are done.

The benefits of true and real teamwork to any organization must be an imperative and a call to action. Organizations that do nothing are going to get left behind.

Imperative 1:

Teamwork and teams are a quintessential element of working life. There are obvious and commonly agreed strengths and advantages that accrue to both the individual and the organization through effective teams. These cannot be realized other than by chance and this is rare, unless organizations take a systematic approach to teamwork, recognize the need for strategy and bring teamwork to the top of the agenda. Anything else is a derogation of opportunity and competitive advantage. The time has come to wake up and smell the coffee.

The gig economy and its implications

The gig economy creates a pressing imperative for teams, team-work and the need for strategy. These are people (giggers) seeking short-term contracts or freelance work as opposed to permanent employment. The gig economy has always been with us but has risen to popular consciousness in recent times. Essentially, with the advent of online platforms as marketplaces for freelancers and the self-employed to source and bid for work, the contingency workforce has been re-labelled the gig economy. This is based on the idea that each piece of work an individual secures is akin to an individual gig. Many will be aware of the term for more negative reasons, associating the gig economy with recent court cases where individuals and groups sought better conditions and workers' rights similar to those of full-time employees. Regard-less of how one views it or labels it, the gig economy is here to stay and the numbers choosing to work in the gig economy are rising exponentially.

Giggers now represent 16% of the UK workforce, having doubled in the past four decades, and the numbers continue to rise.[2] Full-time employment in the same period has remained static, indicating that recent business growth has been dependent on the giggers. Figures from the USA suggest that one in three people are now working freelance and this may potentially rise to 50% by the early 2020s.[3] A 2015 Deloitte study of multination-als found 33% of the workforce was on contingency and 51% of leaders believed that this would continue to rise.[4] It is predicted that the UK could reach a 50% contingency workforce by the end of the next decade.[2]

Whether it is a gigger using platforms, a freelancer or self-em-ployed individual using networks, referrals and personal contacts to find work, the contingency workforce is not only here to stay, it is growing rapidly. Whether or not one agrees with the principle of the gig economy, and it has many flaws yet to be worked out, including comparable rights and taxation issues, it is becoming an ever-increasing talent source for organizations. To secure the best and sufficient talent and labour, organizations today must not only access this workforce, they must have a strategy in place to integrate the giggers with their permanent workforce.

This mobile and transient workforce presents a series of challenges to organizations. Now and in the future, they can form part of any workforce. In addition to how these individuals are resourced and recruited, there are also bigger issues of how they are integrated into the organization quickly, how they are motivated and retained, how their productivity is turned on as soon as possible, and how they are held accountable. Giggers matter as much for an employer brand as do full-time employees. Some would even say more so. As they enter and leave short- or medium-term contracts, what they say about their experience can either attract others or turn them off. The online marketplace platforms for giggers are full of feedback on their experiences. The culture of the organization must flex to accommodate what is, and will be, a major element of talent. This includes ensuring that full-time employees understand that giggers are part of the overall workforce and just as important.

The most effective means to the integration of these individuals is through a culture of teaming and teamwork. Teams must be capable of quickly socializing a gigger to the norms of the organization. Teams must have the means to absorb this talent into their routines, and make the gigger feel welcome and needed. Teams must have clear rules of engagement that they can share with an incoming gigger and have clear and unambiguous goals and role clarification to allow the gigger to quickly understand where they fit and where they can contribute in the most effective manner. Team leaders need support and training to help manage and lead these individuals, understanding the key challenges that they bring with them for the team. In such an environment, the issues of psychological safety, maintaining goal clarity and embracing failure as a means of learning and improvement all matter. Team leaders need to be educated to understand these issues and how to manage them effectively.

None of this is possible without a consistent strategy for effective teams and teamwork. The most effective means of managing a contingent workforce, ensuring the benefits are accrued to the organization and the risks are mitigated, is through a teaming culture and a real corporate team strategy.

It has long been accepted that the environment is a major shaper of organizational culture. The giggers are here to stay; 80% plus are gigging out of choice and not necessity.[2] It is a lifestyle choice. They will work for the organizations they believe offer the best opportunities and experience – experience of the work to be done and experience of the culture to be enjoyed, or in some cases to be endured. They can and will walk away from organizations that fail to react and deal with this growing environmental influence. They have the capacity to provide the organization with flexibility, innovation and efficiency, but equally have the capacity to destroy an employer brand where their experience is poor.

The gig economy and its explosive growth is, without question, a major imperative for organizations to get teamwork to the top of the agenda.

Imperative 2:

The gig economy alone is a sufficient imperative for organizations to embrace the need for strategy and develop teaming and teamwork. How else can an organization meet the challenges of this key environmental condition? A failure to do so not only impacts the ability of an organization to resource and retain appropriate and needed talent but can also lead to an employer brand being seriously damaged. Wake up and drink the coffee before it is too late.

Millennials (Generation Y)

There are many implications of the millennials for the work-place. However, one definitive imperative that they bring is for teamwork and a strategy that enables a teaming culture to ensure that organizations fully connect and engage with this generation. Millennials, those born between 1981 and 2000, now account for approximately 40% of the workforce and by 2025 will account for 75% of the workforce.[5] Baby boomers and Generation X – take note.

Millennials have a very different disposition and approach to work than preceding generations. In my view, this can only be met through a teaming culture. They are in a state of ascendancy and will soon become the majority leaders of our organizations, superseding those generations before them. They are already the biggest proportion of the workforce. They will wreak havoc on the traditional hierarchy and means of organization in the minds of many baby boomers or, as the millennials see it, they will make for a better, more streamlined and sensible approach to the world of work. The millennial mindset is very different to that of the baby boomers. Already they are driving change and the baby boomers are struggling to accommodate them. The 'rise of teams' and the network of teams (the new organization of tomorrow) is as much to do with millennials and their demands for a changed workplace as it is being driven by market forces and a demand for an agile workforce.

Older generations perceive their world through the traditional hierarchy. They value money, status, individual work, power and the hierarchy. The traditional hierarchy and all that goes with it is no longer an efficient or effective means of organizational structure. Command and control, chain of command, vertical upward flows of power, perceptions that staff are there to serve the manager and do what they are told, silo management and censured communication, rigid rules and an overall environment of, "Do as I say, not as I do," from the top are what characterize the traditional hierarchy. Some organizations have managed to break this; many more claim to but, in reality, often fall short of their espoused position. The baby boomers, in control for today, really cannot see how things could work otherwise, predominantly because of their values.

Millennials, on the other hand, see the world very differently, often in complete contrast with the baby boomers.

Millennials reject the traditional hierarchy and crave flexibility and collaboration. They are not concerned with titles and status and admire those with experience and knowledge rather than those with position and power. They do not have the same level or need for loyalty of preceding generations, with many expecting to move from organization to organization every two to three years. They want new jobs and assignments every 12 to 24 months and will not wait three to five years for a promotion. They thrive on innovation and change and get bored quickly with the same old, same old. They are drawn to projects that connect to their strengths and abilities and offer learning opportunities. They are constantly seeking new skills to enhance their capability to move from project to project.

They seek as much to enhance their own brand as they do the employer brand, to enable themselves to have the flexibility and capacity to move between projects and organizations. This drives a very different expectation of the manager/subordinate relationship.

They want coaching and not supervision, peer structures and opportunities to interact with various peers and leaders rather than being limited to a single leader or traditional small team. This is very much at odds with baby boomers, who see their roles associated with power and position and the vertical upward power of the traditional hierarchy. Millennials are less concerned with trying to fit in with a culture and more interested in expanded communication, collaboration and flexibility.

Millennials seek not just collaboration in projects but also collaborative open work spaces, to facilitate communication and the sharing of ideas and skills. They want a leader working within the group setting, rather than instructing from a distance.

They are focused on achieving, through personal networks and technology, and not through hierarchies.

They reject entirely outdated annual performance appraisals. They thrive on fairness and performance-based feedback, not tenure and seniority. Feedback in real time, little and often, is what is demanded. It is a requirement for instant gratification, derived from 'the internet of things' (their world), and their immediate access to information of all kinds is now considered the norm. Waiting 12 months for feedback on something is not in their mindset. This demand for immediate feedback is best met by weekly conversations, be that via chat forums, team video conferences or face-to-face meetings. Millennials want meaningful interpersonal work relationships and the regular informal check-in is a critical element of this. This is possible in a teaming culture with leaders co-located with their teams in an open and collaborative environment. The traditional hierarchy does not accommodate this type of communication.

Millennials are without question the single biggest influence on organizational design today. Every organization must find the most appropriate means to accommodate them. The old days of vertical upward power structures are gone. There is only one way to meet the requirements of millennials and that is through teaming and teamwork. Organizations must now accept the inevitable and begin the process of delivering truly team-based organizations. In doing so they will connect and engage with this generation. Remember, this generation will soon take over and drive the change anyway. Those that initiate the change now will create competitive advantage, attract and retain the better talent, and derive the innovation and productivity that are unleashed by a team-based culture.

A team-based culture meets the needs of the millennial. It delivers:

- Collaborative environments;
- Flexibility in role rotation and risk minimization due to absences;
- The richness of project variation;

- Leaders working in the group setting and not directing from a distance;
- The capacity to deliver on real time feedback and communication demands;
- Direct and personal coaching and mentoring, appropriate to an individual's needs;
- Immediate and regular feedback.

A team-based culture will not happen without strategy – a real strategy that delivers a consistent and effective means for teamwork. A strategy that places teaming culture and teamwork at the top of the agenda for all and not just a few in HR or Organizational Development functions. It needs joined-up thinking and a recognition that teaming and teamwork do not happen by magic. Millennials, the biggest percentage of the workforce, are demanding it.

Imperative 3:

Millennials, in their disposition, have created the single biggest factor for the imperative of teams. The organization that fails to address this issue will find itself quickly falling behind in competitiveness and ultimately will be unable to attract and retain the talent it requires. An old Chinese proverb goes: "When the winds of change blow, some build walls, others build windmills." Too many organizations are building walls and not picking up the coffee aroma on the winds of change.

The new organization – designed for purpose

For two years in a row (2016[6] and 2017[7]), Deloitte's Global Human Capital Trends survey has positioned organizational redesign as the number one concern for businesses. In 2016 it termed this 'The Rise of Teams' and in 2017 'The Organization of the Future – Arriving Now'. There is no question that it is a topic of major discussion, but what is actually being done about it?

Agility is a key term used in the new organization. Agile decision making and the agile workforce are the holy grail of the new organization. There is an overall focus on increasing connectivity, communication and collaboration enabled by technology, which are deemed necessary for agility. So, what is driving what? Is the availability of technology driving change regardless of its appropriateness or is there a real need to change to meet the challenges of business?

There appears to be a growing acceptance that the traditional hierarchy is no longer the best means of organizing a business. Flat structures, devolved decision making, team empowerment and collaboration are all viewed as means to create the agile organization: the organization that reacts quickly, meets changing customer needs, drives innovation and continuously adapts to its environment. These are now considered essential for survival.

While I hear the talk, I do not necessarily see the action. There is no question that technology is accelerating. Moore's law (1965), describing a driving force of technological and social change, productivity and economic growth alone, tells us that computing power doubles every 18 to 24 months. We can all see the revolutionary changes to our lives in how we communicate, live, work and share knowledge and information. Although slowing now, this law is still used in the semi-conductor industry to drive research and development targets, and the pace of change is set to continue. Yes, we should embrace these technological advances, but just not for the sake of their availability. They can be, and are in some instances, fantastic tools to enhance business, but they are enablers and enhancers only in the right circumstances. Willy-nilly adopting of technology without first adapting the nature of the organization is, I believe, a fruitless exercise.

HR spend overall is increasing, but I suggest the vast majority of it is on new technology in a mad rush not to get left behind.

Eileen Shapiro in 1995 called this 'fad surfing' in relation to the practice of riding the crest of the latest management craze, pulling out again just in time to ride the next wave – interesting for the project leaders, very lucrative for consultants and very often disastrous for the organization.[8] If organizational redesign is so critical, with 92% of companies surveyed by Deloitte (2016)[6] citing it as their number one challenge, then where is the budget allocation and the spend on organizational redesign?

Throwing technology at the challenge to improve real-time communication and collaboration, and to empower teams in the hope of a more agile organization is not going to work unless the traditional hierarchy is fundamentally changed in favour of a team-based, teaming culture. This is 'cart before the horse' thinking.

Some have made the break, but they are few and far between. Others claim to be fundamentally changing and point to their physical environment of hot desking, encouraging people to work from home and so on, even introducing collaborative work spaces. Excuse a degree of cynicism here. Many of these initiatives have nothing to do with agile workforces, empowerment and teamwork and more to do with cost reduction in terms of facilities spend. The drive to decrease square footage and fixed work positions, along with home working, is about cost and nothing to do with a team-based culture in most instances. Most organizations tend to have open collaborative work spaces that are often not being used. In many instances the organization moves to eradicate these spaces based on low usage after a relatively short period of time. They will never be used if the organization design is a traditional hierarchy and not geared in design terms towards true collaboration.

Organizations must be designed for purpose – function follows form. This means a fundamental rethink of the organization's design and how it interconnects and operates. Traditional hierarchies are not designed to be agile. They are robust, and although they do provide rigid control they are not empowering by their nature. Organizations must now commit resource and budget to this critical element. They have got to build a network of teams if they want agility. They should seek outside help in this, as it is difficult to see the whole picture when you are in the middle of it – 'the woods for the trees' syndrome.

Throwing technology at the existing traditional structure is not going to work. In fact, it can make things worse. How something is designed is how it will work. If you just start attaching things to the existing design it can in fact break it. Throwing new technology, particularly new communication technology, at the traditional hierarchical structure is not a good thing. The traditional organization is not designed to accommodate it. It is like trying to add an engine to a parachute in the hope that you can get the parachute to reverse direction or improve what it has been designed to do.

Before technology must come the design of the new organization. It must be designed for purpose. If a business requires collaboration, innovation, empowerment of teams, cross-functional teams, agile decision making and an agile workforce, then a new design is required. It is not about lip service and espoused positions, it is about real change. It is through such a change in structure that one can then deploy the new technology to enable that new structure. It is not just about tinkering with the existing structure, which is what most do. It is about starting with a blank piece of paper, determining what you do as a business and what organizational design best suits your purpose. Today this is a team-based design.

Organizations must begin the serious business of organizational design change. It does cost money, it does take time and people will resist as change is universally resisted. Career paths will change, power will shift and values held dearly by the baby boomers and Generation X will not only be under threat, but radically altered.

Imperative 4:

To deliver effective teamwork requires a radical change in organizational design. Organizations need to commit as much time and budget to this element in the early stages of change as they do to technology. The right environment and platform must be in place for the technology to deliver its promise. You have to invest in good coffee and a good percolator to get good coffee in the cup.

The need for strategy

So how can an organization address these issues and capitalize on the benefits of effective teams? How does one develop organizations of networked teams: an agile workforce that can not only keep pace with the challenges of a fluid, unpredictable world, but also meets the needs of the new workforce – the giggers and the millennials?

The answer lies in a concept called corporate team strategy (CTS). I work globally on team initiatives across the USA, Europe and the Middle East. From airlines to healthcare, from fast food to financial services, and from pharmaceuticals to technology, I have yet to find an organization with a developed CTS and, more importantly, a deployed strategy for teams. Even though the majority of organizational output is achieved through collaboration, and teamwork is a key element of competitive advantage, few seem to have grasped this vital concept.

A CTS is a strategy separate to all other people strategies. It is about understanding what, why and how teams are deployed into the organization and how they are supported. It is about understanding the difference between team types – traditional, project, teaming work groups (TWGs) and virtual teams. It is about how you select for teams (e.g. are the attributes of team members the same for the traditional team and the virtual team?).

A CTS is about deploying a team assessment methodology and team model that create an environment for reflexivity for teams.

It also creates a structured means for teams to self-assess and make improvements at a team level. It is about creating time and supported space for teams to regularly meet to consider their *modus operandi*. It is about understanding what constitutes good teamwork, what is successful teamwork and setting the benchmark not just in terms of performance but in terms of minimum standards for teams.

A CTS seeks to identify the key business metrics that are impacted by teamwork and can be correlated with a team measure to indicate successful or failing teams in such a way that intervention can happen at the earliest possible moment for a team as required. A CTS can also determine the best approach for team-based assessment integrated with individual performance management.

For too long the assumption has existed that teamwork just happens – we are all naturals when it comes to teamwork. Interventions for teams are for failing teams, when a team gets into trouble. We must accept that all teams can be more effective than they are today. Anything we do for teams must be for all teams and not just a few, from the CEO and their team to every team in the organization.

To do this means developing a CTS and identifying a tool and methodology that supports the team to be self-serving in terms of its onward development. A CTS is a separate strategy but must be integrated with other people strategies, e.g. learning and development, ensuring that the programmes for teams are just that – programmes for teams and not for individuals. A CTS draws support from the Organizational Development function, but with solutions that are specifically geared and designed to suit the team environment. While being interdependent on other people strategies, a successful CTS aims for self-sufficiency in teams in terms of improving their effectiveness. Most teams, if given the time to be reflective and given a reliable, robust and proven methodology, will improve themselves. Research has demonstrated that teams that are reflective are the teams that are innovative.

To begin the process of developing a CTS, **Table 1** outlines some of the questions that must be answered. One would think that this information would be readily accessible, given the importance of teamwork. Most organizations will not be able to answer these questions without detailed research. If a team-based organization is what one wants, then these answers are essential. Developing the strategies, processes and programmes to deliver on these concerns is what ultimately delivers a CTS.

Table 1.
Questions to be addressed in formulating a CTS

1	How important is teamwork in our organization?	11	Are there differences in performance between teams?
2	Are employees engaged in more than one team at a time?	12	Is there a team that demonstrates the ideal for our organization?
3	How many teams do we have at any one time?	13	What are the team work behaviours we expect of teams?
4	How many team types do we have at any one time – traditional, project, TWGs, virtual, committee?	14	How do we measure team success?
5	What is the optimal team size in terms of team type?	15	Is there a means of assessment?
6	When do we deploy these different types of teams?	16	How often do we assess teams?
7	What is our model for teamwork?	17	How often do teams assess their own effectiveness?
8	What is our language of teams/teaming?	18	Is teamwork performance integrated with individual performance?
9	What tools do we provide to support our teams?	19	What training do we provide for team members and leaders?
10	What kind of leadership do these different teams need?	20	Who do teams turn to when they need help?

As one develops a CTS, one is impacting the culture of the organization. Culture can be described in simple terms as 'how we do things around here' or can be observed in the way the employee body works day-to-day. As a CTS develops in content and sophistication over time, so does 'the way we do things around here'. The culture changes from a traditional hierarchy to a team-based teaming culture. The organization is redesigning itself. It is not easy, it takes time, effort, expertise and budget, but it is not rocket science.

Despite the increase in HR spend globally on systems and technology, despite the overall spend and ever-increasing deployment of new technology, business productivity has not grown or kept pace with technological progress. Growth in business productivity is at its lowest since the 1970s.[9] In part I suggest this is because we are imposing technology on organizations to deliver something that the traditional hierarchy cannot do. It is like putting wings on the family car and assuming it can fly!

When the strategy is in place, when there is a proven methodology and tool to support the teams, and when reflexivity is a reality, team effectiveness will improve, innovation will increase, and team morale and motivation will continue to build. The new technologies will have a real impact on productivity and will be fit for purpose, as will the design of the organization and the emerging culture. The traditional hierarchy has had its day. The new organization is arriving and a focus on developing a CTS is a big step on the way to delivering that new world.

Imperative 5:
Successful teamwork is not easy. It takes hard
work, persistence and commitment, and it most
certainly takes a well-crafted CTS, but it is not rocket
science. To address the issues of a CTS is to begin
the process of organizational redesign, which, over
time, leads to an enhanced culture. Is that not reason enough to consider that the time for teams is
now? The rise of teams is inexorable and cannot be
avoided; those who get ahead of the game will stay
ahead. Wake up, the coffee has been percolating
for some time now.

Chapter 2.

Debunking some myths

Myths
Fables, legends, folklore – more aptly described in terms of teams as fallacies, falsehoods or cock-and-bull stories.

There are many common perceptions in the world of work teams. It is difficult to know how some of these have come about and why they are so ingrained in people's thinking. Unfortunately, most of them are at best inaccurate and, in many instances, simply wrong. These perceptions distort the approach to teamwork and undermine most efforts to develop teams.

Having spent many years supporting work teams I have developed a strong aversion to these myths. They have become my 'soap box' issues on teamwork.

Team development and teamwork are fun

This is a belief that is misguided, misinformed and simply wrong.

When discussing team development with clients, one issue is constantly hovering over the entire discussion and it is the question of fun.

It starts with the question, "Is what you do fun?" and continues with "It will be great to give the team a good day out – they work so hard and are struggling. It will be a bit of a reward for them." Invariably the reason I am brought in to help is because the team is struggling and overtly so. The last thing they need is a day of fun. They need to address the issues that are causing concern.

The reality is that teamwork – and, more importantly, effective teamwork – requires hard work, consistent effort and continuous attention. When the same organization is buying IT training, sales training or management development the first question is not, "Is it fun?" There is little concern as to whether the project management training course is fun. There is more of a concern with the content and whether the programme delivers proficiency in project management. Nobody expects the role of finance, sales or production to be fun but, for some reason, when you mention teams and team development, fun comes to the top of the agenda.

The fact that it can be an enjoyable experience to work in an effective team should not be confused with it being fun. If the team wants fun, absolutely, they can go out for an evening of bowling, five-a-side football, a meal – these are good things to do and they can be fun, but do not confuse them with the hard work required to develop and maintain an effective team.

Bear in mind that people often resent having to give up their free time, family time, personal time for supposed 'team development' events. When offsite events are organized (with the best intentions) they can be very stressful for some members of the team. Not everyone enjoys physical activity. Many are embarrassed to be asked to perform such activities, and do not like to wear casual clothes in front of colleagues or indeed share life stories, which have all become common in team programmes. To force them to participate or to find an excuse for not attending can have a very negative impact. What one person considers fun is excruciating and painful for another.

I believe the idea that teams and teamwork should be fun stems from our involvement in team games in our spare time and indeed in watching our favourite teams playing professional sport. Both of these activities are great fun for us as individuals. We do them because they are our hobbies and we take great enjoyment (or great sadness when our team loses) from them and the relaxed social environment they provide. That said, and speaking from personal experience, when I was younger, turning up for training with my local football team on a wet and cold November Tuesday evening was not fun. Yes, there was a sense of camaraderie, a sense of purpose, but it involved a serious commitment and sacrifice. This was a personal choice, wholly voluntary, and I had the option to withdraw at any time without any repercussions other than potentially to my pride. These are not the conditions that surround a work team, and this is worth noting.

Myth 1 debunked:
**Teamwork is not fun. Effective teamwork requires
sustained and continuous effort and can be enjoyable
when effective and successful, but this should not be
confused with fun. The guiding requirement for team
development initiatives must be the capacity of the
chosen approach to deliver higher performing teams,
addressing the challenges and issues the team is
facing and not the initiative's capacity for fun. You have
got to pick the right coffee for the right occasion.**

Sports teams and work teams – apples and oranges

The continuous comparison between sports teams and work
teams is complete nonsense. This is particularly true when
the comparison is drawn with a professional sports team. Too
often I see bigger organizations enlisting the manager or coach
of a successful professional team as a motivational speaker on
teamwork. While these individuals are interesting and draw the
crowd because of their fame, there is little they can tell you about
the motivation of an average work team as there is no logical
comparison to be made – apples and oranges. There is no benefit
in comparing professional sports teams and work teams. They do
not operate or succeed in the same manner.

Let me give the example of a professional football team and
consider the differences in **Table 2** (next page).

If, however, you do want to make comparisons between work
teams and sports teams, I recommend that you go to your local
park on a Saturday morning and observe the 'under nines' football team in action. The chaos, the disorganization and the sight
of 20 players chasing the ball at the same time in one corner of
the field are far more representative of a work team than anything a professional sports team does.

Table 2.
Comparison of a professional football team and a work team

Professional football team	Work team
Networks of talent scouts track talent internationally, from an early age. Teams buy players with a very specific role in mind – striker, defender, goalkeeper. Obscene amounts of money are paid in transfer fees and subsequently obscene amounts of money are paid as 'wages'.	For the most part, work teams are inherited by their leaders and must make do with what they get. When new teams are formed, they are realistically put together based on who is available with some politics thrown in for good measure. Apart from some CEOs and a few bankers, we do not pay in the millions for these team members.
Professional teams spend 99% of their time practising and planning what they do and only 1% doing what they do. They dissect the opposition, complete vast amounts of research, review games and track every move, kick and step a player makes during a game and in training.	Work teams are action and task-oriented, do not practise and indeed most do not give sufficient, if any, time to planning and evaluation.
Motivation in a professional team stems from very different sources. Apart from the money (yes, money can be a motivator), players do their job in front of thousands of adoring fans, who praise their every move and even support them when things go wrong.	Work teams are seldom observed in the work situation, rarely get external feedback of any sort (unless it is negative), and I have yet to see a work team perform in front of a supporting and cheering audience.
Team members are supported in every aspect of their work life, by dieticians, doctors and physios, as well as through luxury transportation and hotels. They don't have to submit expenses claims and they are paid for endorsing brands or given expensive presents to endorse a brand. They are mollycoddled.	Work teams receive little support day-to-day. Sometimes, they may even find it hard to find a meeting room. Any expenses must go through an exhaustive process with the team member, more often than not, having paid out the expenses first then reclaiming it. They seldom have any budgetary control at the team level, despite the overt claim by the organization that, "Of course we trust our employees." Work teams are more likely treated with disdain and are certainly not mollycoddled.
Professional teams have clear goals – win the championship, for example – and due to continuous research have a clear understanding of the challenges facing them in each game, broken down to an individual level with a strategy developed to tackle each challenge. They have clear means of assessing performance for each team member.	Work teams seldom know what is facing them and often must meet challenges head on, reacting in real time. Team members are not prepared in any way resembling the approach of professional teams to meet challenges. There is little, if any, team performance evaluation and seldom is team output tied to any business metric.

Myth 2 debunked:

Sports teams and work teams are not the same and continuous comparison between the two is, for the most part, meaningless. There is one lesson that can be learned – the 99:1 ratio of practice and planning for what you do. Teams that give more time to reflection, planning and evaluation will be far more effective than those that do not. Stop bringing in speakers who cannot connect meaningfully with your teams. It only leads to unfulfilled expectations. Do not serve cold coffee.

Team building at offsite events takes time away from real work

Suggest a team-building session and immediately the outdoors springs to mind. Contrary to popular opinion, I am convinced outdoor events do not help in delivering an effective team. There are many variations of this with some even run by ex-special forces soldiers. Primarily they are based on the completion of group exercises and challenges, supposedly developing team spirit and team effectiveness.

Every team member is encouraged to participate equally by the facilitator and the work team leader no longer has the same level of power as this is ceded to the facilitator. The team are given clear and precise goals and directions. This is not the norm at work. The degree of psychological safety is higher at these events (controlled by the facilitator) and everyone's opinion tends to be heard. No idea is considered too wacky as most of the tasks are wacky in the first place. Credit for new ideas and novel solutions is given as the ideas are developed. The team becomes increasingly successful at the tasks as the day progresses, based on this more engaged way of interacting.

When they return to the workplace they are faced with the leader reasserting their control again, not being heard, lack of clear goals and roles, suggestions and solutions being knocked, and ideas being stolen.

What is actually happening at these outdoor events?

The number one problem with these sessions is their capacity to create an expectation that the team can work better together. The sessions are carefully constructed – I know because I used to deliver them at one time – and precise instructions are given for each exercise along with clear objectives. For starters, this is not the norm in the workplace. Often the exercises bear no resemblance to any work-related task that the team carry out. As the day progresses the tasks may get more difficult but most teams complete the tasks successfully because they are designed to be completed successfully.

The outcome is a team that are in high spirits and delighted with themselves in their success. They are full of energy and drive to get back to the workplace and prove their effectiveness with this new-found capacity to work together. But, when they get back to work, lo and behold nothing has changed. If fact, very quickly the frustration levels rise as the team members recall how well they worked together offsite, but just cannot make it happen at work. Often the very opposite of what was intended becomes reality. The team are less effective and more fractious.

The offsite is a false environment. Not only do the tasks not represent the normal work of the team, but the conditions in which they happen are also not representative!

Real team development that delivers sustainable progression and effectiveness happens in the workplace. Teams that take time to think about how they do things rather than what they do can always develop more effective means of working together. Teams that address goal and role clarity, planning and evaluation, composition and structure, appropriate leadership style and participation, conflict management and performance recognition, and communication and trust are the teams that will not only deliver more but will also create a psychologically safe environment as a platform for their effectiveness. All of this takes place in the workplace and not in the outdoors or at wild and wonderful offsite events.

Myth 3 debunked:
Team development is not about time away from real work. Rather it is about correctly giving time to reflection on 'how' the team does things, rather than 'what' it does. It can and does take place in normal work hours, where it is far more effective and does not serve to embarrass or compromise any team member. Think carefully before organizing any outdoor/offsite events in terms of the team members and their various dispositions. Remember, it is not about fun; it is about addressing the real issues that drive team effectiveness. Do not provide tea when they need coffee.

Team development is only for 'problem teams'

No, it is not. Every team, regardless of level, composition and seniority (yes even the CEO and their team), can do better than they are doing today. Every team has room for improvement, but they must give time for reflection away from the day-to-day on a regular basis to think about how they do what they do. When choosing a team for development, companies will invariably pick a team in trouble, a team that is failing. While what I do will work for this team, I often ask for a company's best performing team. If I can make that team even better, it is clear what I can do for the failing team.

A world-leading consumer brand chose a particularly impaired team at the outset of my engagement. I asked why the team was failing and was told categorically that the leader was the problem. The leader was incapable of leading the team and this had become obvious over time. This is a 'head in the sand' scenario that I come across a lot. The company knew what the problem was. They also knew the correct solution but were not prepared to implement it. Why would they think I could fix the problem of a totally unsuitable leader? There is a very simple answer – replace the leader. This situation is such a failure of leadership and common sense that it beggars description.

The reality is that there are many 'problem' teams that should never be developed. When a team is failing it will be because they have failed to address the core issues of team effectiveness. Invariably, this is a team leader concern. The team relies on the team leader to ensure that such issues are addressed. If the team leader is not capable of doing so, they are in effect incapable of leading the team. If the issue is with team members and poor performance and/or negative behaviour, it also falls back on the leader to deal with the issues. A failing team, for whatever reason, is related to the leader or the leader's leader and their approach. For me it is one of the first places to look in addressing the problem. There may well be other issues, such as the leader's leader disempowering the leader or the team being set up without any real purpose (it happens), but the leader has to be the first port of call in a failing team scenario.

Team development is perceived as something that one does for failing teams. The smart organization will recognize that all teams need to commit to their own development. Remember that 90% of what is done in an organization happens through collaborative effort. Failure to recognize this is a failure of strategy and, ultimately, a failure of leadership.

Myth 4 debunked:

Team development is for all teams, all the time. If this approach is adopted then there will be far fewer teams in trouble, which is often only recognized once it is too late. Can you imagine an organization that could drive 10% to 20% improvement in team effectiveness across the organization and the impact this will have on the bottom line? This can only happen if there is belief that all teams can be better and have a continuous means of improvement, development and measurement. Coffee is for everyone, not just the few.

Teams are there to support their leader

Nothing could be further from the truth and the converse is the needed reality – leaders are there to support their teams. This is what is referred to as the inverted hierarchy. Leaders are at the bottom of the pyramid, supporting those in the team above them and not the other way around. This is a 'get over it already' moment. As a team leader, the only means you have to success is in the success of your team. The more successful they are, the more success for you. Your job is to get all the barriers to team performance out of the way. Your job is to deliver strategy and structure for the team, and it is the team that deliver output, quality and customer satisfaction.

Team leadership is about creating the confidence in your team members to follow you by anticipating their needs and ensuring that all that can be done to enable each member of the team is done – so they can deliver. A key leadership task is to organize the team to be self-managing and as much as possible to be self-directing. This means fostering collaboration within the team and also requires the team leader to have the confidence to let go and empower the team at an individual level. The alternative is that you as leader do everything, believing that you have all the answers, and the rest of the team becomes your audience while you perform.

Motorola in its heyday really got this principle. It believed the most important people in a manufacturing plant were the operators, or the 'direct workforce' as they were referred to. These were the people who made the product and produced wealth for the company. The managers and leaders were called the 'indirect workforce' and were viewed as a cost centre and overhead. They did not produce wealth – they consumed it. As a Motorola HR manager in the 1980s, it was more than my job was worth to allow the ratio in my plant to deviate from the 80:20 rule. The workforce had to be 80% direct (wealth creators) and only 20% indirect (overhead). The indirect workforce had one guiding principle – make sure that there was no impediment of any form to an operator's capacity to generate wealth. This in my view should be every team leader's preoccupation. How do I ensure that the team are able to operate at their fullest capacity? What is in their way that I can fix? How can I help every team member to do their job?

Myth 5 debunked:
Team leaders are there to support their teams and not the other way around. The only way a team leader can be successful is through the success of their team. The leader is at the bottom of the structure supporting the team – the inverted hierarchy. By the way, I believe this to be true for leaders at all levels in the organization, even the CEO. The leaders need to make the coffee, not the more junior team members.

Harmony is essential – conflict is anathema

Conflict is not the issue; it is how the conflict is managed that causes problems. Conflict is essential in a team. It is the source of innovation. Imagine a team that does not argue, debate and disagree at times. What hope does it have to innovate, find better ways to do things or address problems and failures? How can a team possibly learn together if it doesn't have conflict? A team without conflict would be a very ineffectual team.

Chapter 13 deals with this issue in much more detail, but for now appreciate the fact that harmony is nice to have, but conflict is essential. How you manage conflict is the critical element in this equation. Conflict can never be allowed to become personalized. There must be rules of engagement. There must be someone (normally the leader) acting as a facilitator to ensure that all ideas, disagreements and debates are encouraged and resolved to the benefit of the team moving forward. If you have a team that exists in perfect harmony, you had better introduce debate, solicit differences of opinion and get the team talking about different ways of doing things. Stir it up a bit or the team will be going nowhere.

I recently worked with a team in London who did not 'do conflict'. The team members did not see the need for it. It was a critical analytics team providing essential data to the business. All seven members of the team were PhDs and they believed in reason, logic and data – conflict was unprofessional and unnecessary. Their team profile clearly indicated that there was a considerable difference of opinion on a critical element of their psychological safety.

I asked them to discuss this difference. They were reluctant and said that there was no issue in the team. The team's average response was above the average and, therefore, they could see no problem. As a group they had answered this question on their psychological safety with a clear lack of consensus and had done so in the past couple of hours. This was current and not historical data.

Eventually they took up the conversation and indeed there was no issue within the team. There was, however, a serious issue between the team and the rest of the organization, which often did not like the message the team delivered through their analytical data. They felt at times that their message was treated dismissively and they were being ridiculed. Their psychological safety was seriously undermined in these situations and they did not have a strategy for dealing with it. This often meant they dumbed down or softened the message they delivered, with obvious negative impact for the business. Following heartfelt debate and argument, they came up with a strategy to support each other in these situations and went away comfortable and confident that they could now deliver any message without fear. Without the argument and debate this would not have happened and both the company and the team would have suffered continuing negative consequences.

It is conflicts of ideas, approaches and solutions that matter. Personalized conflict is anathema and must be quickly eradicated.

Myth 6 debunked:
Harmony is nice to have, but conflict is essential. It is all about the way conflict is managed that determines a positive or negative outcome. This requires rules of engagement, planning and evaluation. Yes, this means thinking about 'how' you do things, not just 'what' you do as a team. Not everyone drinks the same coffee.

Organizations and senior leaders are champions of teamwork

The rhetoric tends to indicate this as fact – the reality, however, points to a very different scenario.

Organizations will openly profess their belief in teams and many include teamwork as one of their core values. They will speak about collaboration, openness and how much they trust their employees.

When one looks a little closer, the gaps emerge. I have yet to find an organization with a genuine and real team strategy. There is a strategy for everything else, but not one for teams. Most organizations cannot tell you how many teams they have in play. They have no idea as to the number of each type they have – traditional, project, TWG or virtual teams. There is little recognition that different teams require different approaches to recruitment and composition. For example, the virtual team requires very different types of people in terms of membership to the traditional team. All team types have strengths and weaknesses, and all have different challenges. Yet, no strategy exists to deal with these differences. No standards are established as a minimum requirement for an effective team and equally no metrics are in place to understand what constitutes success for a team in an organization. Where is the integration of individual performance management and team performance? Who do teams go to if they need team support, not individual coaching or learning and development?

I could go on and on about the things not done in terms of teams from an organizational perspective. Teamwork does not happen by accident. The organization, for the most part, operates through teams, yet all the systems and processes are designed for the individual – recruitment, compensation, performance management and general support. The disposition of most organizations would suggest they believe in magic and that a team will be high performing simply by the virtue of being created. For teams to work and the real return to be realized, an organization must put a CTS in place.

Effective teamwork requires empowered teams. Teams must be given the power to perform, as well as the responsibility to perform. In many instances, this is anathema to a senior leader as it requires them to cede control to the team. Despite having come up through the ranks and often complained about this very phenomenon, they replicate the behaviour, further embedding it in the culture and undermining the teams involved. When a team fails to deliver, it is the team's fault and this serves as a justification in the leader's mind for their behaviour in the first place. A disempowered team cannot succeed. This issue starts at the top and often permeates down the organization as behaviour is reinforced.

Even worse is the concept I call 'longarmitis'. This is where the senior leader cannot resist opportunities to reach into the teams two, three and even four levels beneath them in the hierarchy. This is the CEO who observes an issue in the day-to-day running of the organization and, instead of going to the direct report who has the responsibility for the team, reaches in themselves and address the issue.

This has two immediate and debilitating impacts. Firstly, it completely undermines the direct report and, if done continuously, impedes their ability to manage the teams beneath them. The teams know the CEO will intervene and now wait for that to happen. Secondly, and more importantly, it drives a more damaging dynamic. Where senior leaders are known to do this, the team leaders at every level start to hoard information, double check every decision that their team makes and interfere in the most basic of decisions just in case, because they do not want to appear unaware if a more senior leader reaches in. This sees the team members at various levels abdicating responsibility for any decision making, as they are aware that all decisions are checked and many countermanded. Yet again, the competency of the teams is questioned by their leaders and the justification for intervening by the leader further reinforced in their own minds, only now it is happening at the lower levels as well.

When a team fails or gets into trouble, the first question should be, is the leader or the leader's leader the source of the problem?

Myth 7 debunked:

Despite the rhetoric, organizations and senior leaders
are not the champions of teamwork. In many cases,
their own sense of inadequacy and sense of threat from
an effective team beneath them drives some very negative behaviour that is counterproductive to the team
environment. Organizations and senior leaders must
put these myths to bed and seriously question their own
behaviour. The time has come. I think they really prefer
hot chocolate to coffee, but are not telling anyone.

Chapter 3.

Topical concerns

> **Topical**
> *Immediate relevance, important owing to its applicability to current events. Teamwork is on a change curve and it is shifting rapidly.*

As any subject develops focus and interest, there will always be several hot topics that emerge and grab attention. The organization, team leaders and team members intent on developing teamwork should be aware of these topics, seek to understand them and take on board the thinking that develops as teamwork experts discuss and argue these important elements. There are six equally important hot topics that need to be carefully considered and understood by all involved in teamwork and, ultimately, incorporated into any developing team strategy or CTS.

Team size

Size does matter after all! The issue of team size has been debated on and off for many years. It does seem to be a topic that organizations ignore or, at the very least, brush over. There is substantial evidence that team size has a great impact on the effectiveness of a team in a work context. Let me be very clear and say there is no consensus on actual size but, if one considers the large body of research out there, the accepted range for team size is somewhere between three and twelve – two is a pair or dyad and not a team in a work context. For me the fundamental rule is no double digits and most of the research supports this position. That is not to say that one will not find many so-called teams in the workplace of up to 20 people. These are not teams but groups, and the likelihood is that these large groups will comprise two or more actual teams.

The issue of team size is linked to how we define a team and indeed to the way the term 'team' is used and understood. The term is applied generically and seems to encompass all group activity, often being used to refer to an entire department – as in the finance team or the HR team – and, in some instances, an entire company. These larger groups, mistakenly called teams, are in fact composed of many teams. This may seem pedantic of me, but the use of language is important. The term 'team' should only be used to refer to a real team, which by my definition is:

A group of people, normally fewer than ten, that need to work together to achieve a common goal, normally with a single leader and where there is a high degree of interdependence between the team members to achieve the goal or goals.

This issue of definition is a prerequisite of a CTS and each organization needs to arrive at its own agreed definition of a team and stop using the term generically for all groups regardless of size.

While I say no double digits in terms of team size, there are many experts who advocate a much smaller number. Dr Meredith Belbin, a world-renowned expert on teams, advocates four as the ideal number and is comfortable with six, but clearly states in his work that a number higher than this can lead to feelings of redundancy and members feeling less engaged.[10] He also believes an even number encourages consensus decision making and minimizes the issue associated with a casting vote and the propensity for cliques to develop. Others advocate an uneven number, suggesting that decision making can be improved when the team cannot be equally divided. Jeff Bezos, founder and CEO of Amazon, is famously accredited with the two-pizza rule for teams. If it takes more than two pizzas to feed the team, then the team is too big. As far back as 1970, Richard Hackman (an eminent scholar on teamwork) and Neil Vidmar completed a study that suggested that the ideal number was 4.6.[11] Hackman, in his later work and in subsequent interviews about his work, stated that excessive team size is the most common and worst impediment to effective collaboration.

There are many others commenting on team size and the consensus is strong on single digits in terms of team size and the implications for team effectiveness.

There are a number of real issues that have been identified when a team size goes into double digits, namely social loafing, cognitive limitations and the communication overhead. These are in addition to the issue of larger teams breaking down into sub-teams and the inevitable emergence of cliques, which can be very damaging not only to effectiveness but also to interpersonal relationships.

Social loafing: People in larger teams perform less well than those in smaller teams. This was first noted back in the 1860s by French agricultural engineer Maximilien Ringelmann, who discovered that the more people who pulled on a rope, the less effort each individual contributed. This is also true of the work team. Larger teams allow for the concept of social loafing as accountability lessens and people feel less responsibility. Motivation is also impacted, as effort declines with the growing temptation that someone else will pick up the slack. The larger team will always carry passengers, and this can have a very negative impact for all concerned. This is apart from the fact it is simply not a good use of people resources. Social loafing is a real reason to limit team size.

Cognitive limitations: Robin Dunbar, a British anthropologist and evolutionary psychologist, provided further evidence for the limitation of team size. His research considered the relationship between human neocortex size and group size.[12] He determined that there is a limit to the number of individuals with whom any one person can maintain stable relationships and this, he asserted, is a direct function of relative neocortex size. The bottom line is that while we can form a higher number of stable interpersonal relationships than other species, there are limits. Once this number moves into double digits, it becomes more and more difficult to maintain these relationships, and the demand on our time and the effort in maintaining them impact our effectiveness for the task at hand. It appears that our nature and biology are major factors in maintaining effective group activity.

Communication overhead: This is the big one for me. The more members in a team, the more communication channels

required to keep the team informed. A team of 5 people requires
10 conversations to be fully connected and informed. This rises
to 45 for a team of 10, and 91 for a team of 14. If you don't
believe me, do the math with the following formula:

$$[n*(n-1)]/2$$

This is the number in the team multiplied by the number in
the team minus one, divided by two. **Figure 1** demonstrates the
exponential rise in communication channels required as the team
increases in membership. This infers that team members cannot be
adequately informed and, therefore, cannot be fully effective. There
is only so much time in the day. The bigger the team, the more
time required for communication, to the detriment of the tasks to
be completed. Without a doubt, for me this issue is an absolute
imperative for maintaining team size in single digits.

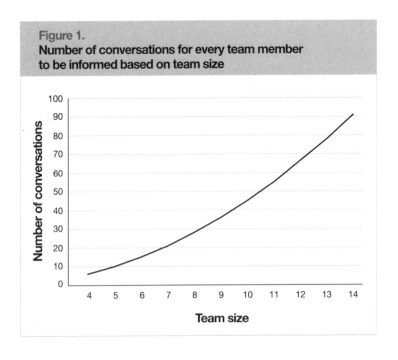

Figure 1.
**Number of conversations for every team member
to be informed based on team size**

A lack of clear definition of what constitutes a team does lead to bigger groups being labelled with the term and, once applied, the expectation is that the group will perform as a team, delivering all the advantages of a team. The subsequent failure of the so-called team to deliver on these expectations has implications for relationships in the group and drives an overall sense of frustration. Managers have a tendency to believe that bigger teams are better, as some sort of contingency strategy to cover for absenteeism. CEOs are particularly prone to over staffing their top team for fear of exclusion, for political reasons, or even the belief that the more direct reports they have, the more information they can control. In the book *Senior Leadership Teams*, Wageman, Nunes, Burruss and Hackman (2008) analysed more than 100 senior executive teams and found only 10% could agree on the actual number of people in the team.[13] There is often a debate as to who is on the team or not and even who should be on the team or removed from the team. If you cannot even determine the right composition of the team, where are you at?

Topic 1:

Size does matter and smaller is better. Larger teams struggle to complete tasks, are less effective, require too much effort in attempts to remain informed and suffer from decreased individual effort. Decision making becomes bogged down in the larger team with cliques forming and entrenched positions being adopted. Organizations today must count the coffee beans and recognize that effective teams come in single-digit numbers. It is an imperative to limit team size.

Psychological safety

Psychological safety has emerged as a hot topic as a basis for developing and operating the ideal or most effective team.

In a psychosocially safe team, members do not suffer the negative consequences of speaking up, expressing a new idea and openly seeking new ways to improve the team or company. Team members enjoy equality of air time, are encouraged to contribute and are not at risk of being ridiculed. These teams remove a team member's need for self-preservation and others' impression management of themselves. In some (many) teams, to ask questions is to appear ignorant, to admit weakness is to appear incompetent, to offer ideas is to appear intrusive and to criticize the status quo is to appear negative. In such an environment, it is better to stay quiet. The individual protects themselves through impression management, but the overall effectiveness of the team is greatly diminished. The converse is true of the team operating in a psychologically safe environment.

In the past few years, Google set out to identify what makes a perfect team and concluded that psychological safety is the number one feature of the effective team, regardless of the team's composition.[14] It found that the essence of effective teamwork is 'how' the team works together – the group's behavioural norm. It identified five key elements, but psychological safety was number one. These findings have been widely publicized and Google's interest in the team debate is a major factor in psychological safety becoming a hot topic today.

Historical context

The concept was first explored in the 1960s by notable academics Edgar Schein (organizational culture) and Warren Bennis (leadership studies), who suggested that psychological safety was important to enable people's sense of security and their capability to adapt their behaviour in dealing with changing organizational challenges. Schein later noted that by helping individuals to overcome defensiveness and anxiety when confronted with situations that contradict their expectations, psychological safety frees them to focus on collective goals and problem prevention rather than self-preservation.

In 1990 William Kahn gave us the first formal definition of employee engagement and argued that psychological safety impacts an individual's readiness to "employ or express themselves physically, cognitively and emotionally during role performance" and not "withdraw and defend their personal selves".[15]

It can even be suggested that the concept was known as far back as the work of Kurt Lewin (1890-1947) in his work on group dynamics.[16] Since then, the principles of evolutionary psychology have been applied to group dynamics. People are perceived to evolve and adapt to increasingly complicated social environments, developing ever-increasing sophistication in their mechanisms for dealing with status, reciprocity, identifying cheaters, ostracism, altruism, group decision making, leadership and intergroup relations.

Probably the most well-known contemporary behavioural scientist credited for bringing this concept to the mainstream is Professor Amy Edmondson of Harvard. She has been researching and writing on the subject since the mid-1990s and her TEDx Talk (2014) presents a very concise summary of her arguments on psychological safety in teams.[17]

Edmondson defines psychological safety as "a belief that one will not be punished or humiliated for speaking up with ideas, questions, concerns or mistakes." She further states that the greater the degree of uncertainty and interdependence in a team's tasks and environment, the greater the need for psychological safety.

The concept is not new or revolutionary. It is, however, enjoying a renaissance.

Psychological safety – chicken or egg?

The current commentators agree on a common theme that psychological safety is the critical starting point for effective teamwork. While they acknowledge that there are other elements required, including compelling goals, structure and clarity, the inference is that psychological safety is the number one priority. Edmondson and Google are probably the most widely recognized commentators in this area and both offer suggestions and steps for creating psychological safety. Edmondson determines the steps as:

1. Frame work as learning problems, as opposed to execution problems – take small steps, learn quickly and move to scale.
2. Acknowledge your own fallibility as a team leader – recognize uncertainty, that one person does not have all the answers and everyone's participation is required in speaking up.
3. Model curiosity by asking a lot of questions – leaders are critical in setting the example.

Edmondson considers the issues along x and y axes, with psychological safety on the x axis and motivation and accountability along the y axis. Based on four quadrants, she sees the high-performing team as having equal consideration for both psychological safety, and motivation and accountability.[17]

Google, on the other hand, albeit heavily influenced by Edmondson, suggests that psychological safety is the number one concern and number one priority. It has developed a five-step model:

1. Psychological safety – team members feel safe enough to take risks and be vulnerable.
2. Dependability – team members get things done on time and meet Google's high bar for excellence.
3. Structure and clarity – team members have clear roles, plans and goals.
4. Meaning – work is personally important to team members.
5. Impact – team members think their work matters and creates change.[14]

In an article in *The Journal of Oncology Practice* titled "Moving Toward Improved Teamwork in Cancer Care: The Role of Psychological Safety in Team Communication" (2016), it was stated: "We focus on psychological safety because a growing body of research on organizations and teams suggests that it is a critical starting ingredient for effective communication and teamwork."[18]

Without doubt the current thinking suggests that psychological safety is the number one priority and that is where one starts.

I agree that psychological safety is important, but I am not so sure that it is the starting point. Teamwork is a complicated process and effective teamwork takes time and effort. I am convinced that psychological safety is an end product, a desired state that the team works towards by ensuring the other critical elements of effective teams are addressed and maximized. A focus on these elements is what creates the platform for a psychologically safe operating environment for the team.

Psychological safety is a condition the team arrives at, be it high or low, because of other factors. Working on these other factors is what creates the understanding, platform and environment for psychological safety to become a reality.

The teams that regularly reflect on 'how' they do things, and address the 12 themes of an effective team, are the teams that build a psychologically safe environment that drives their effectiveness. All 12 themes matter for team effectiveness and, therefore, for psychological safety. These will be looked at in depth in Part 3 of this book; namely these are:

- Goal and role clarity;
- Leadership behaviour and participation;
- Commitment and communication;
- Planning and evaluation;
- Recognition and conflict;
- Composition and organization.

Topic 2:

Psychological safety is a critical factor, an imperative in team effectiveness. It is highly dependent on the disposition of the team leader, as are many of the factors in effective teams. It is, however, a somewhat nebulous concept and can only really be addressed through more tangible factors of team effectiveness, over which the team have control and can be enabled by a progressive team leader. It is time for the organization to 'sense' the coffee and ensure that team leaders

and members are educated in this critical aspect of teamwork. A robust CTS will help address this concern and ensure consistency of approach.

Reflexivity

Reflexivity is a buzzword at present in the world of work teams. It is regularly written about and there have been a number of academic papers on the subject. It can be defined in a team context as the extent to which a team collectively reflects on the team's objectives, strategies and processes, as well as its wider organizations and environments, and makes changes accordingly *or* as a conscious process of reflection essential to team learning. Bottom line: teams need to take time out from the day-to-day to think about and discuss not just 'what' they do but 'how' they do it. The 'how' is the most critical element for me in this process.

The consensus is that teams that are reflective and commit regular time to this process have better co-ordination, clearer communication, better understanding of each other and better shared meanings. They develop common expectations of their actions, are better aligned and interconnected, and suffer less from conflict and misunderstandings. Reflexive teams are simply more innovative and more effective.

There is no question in my mind, or indeed in the research, that, in demanding and challenging times, teams must be continually innovative to maintain and enhance effectiveness and ultimately organizational competitiveness. Teams must be proactive in terms of innovation and not passively reactive. Schippers et al., in a paper published in *The Journal of Management* in 2015, identified a causal effect between workload and reflexivity where higher levels of both within a team deliver higher levels of innovation.[19]

All of the evidence points to a value in reflexivity for teams. It makes sense. A team cannot improve, other than by accident, if time is not committed to understanding the gap between the ideal and current circumstances – that's real scheduled time on a regular basis. Why then is it that most teams commit no time to this vital element of effective teamwork? In fact, most teams that I encounter have seldom, and very often never, taken time out of the day-to-day to think about not only 'what' they do but, more importantly, 'how' they do what they do.

Table 3. Reflexivity schedule based on team type		
Team type	**Description**	**Minimum reflexivity schedule**
Traditional team	Stable, together over time, functionally oriented as in HR, sales or finance teams	Quarterly for between 2 and 4 hours
Project team	Problem solving, innovative, change oriented, short term and often cross functional	Fortnightly for 30 minutes to 1 hour
Teaming work group	Permanent in functional terms with constantly changing composition / membership	Quarterly for between 4 and 8 hours
Virtual team	Can be traditional or project based, rarely a TWG, but not co-located and often geographically spread out with little face-to-face contact	Monthly for between 1 and 2 hours

Reflexivity requires scheduled time out on a regular basis. A regular basis is defined by the team in terms of its needs and by team type. I recommend the following as a minimum.

Reflexivity is a process and needs to be managed as such. It must be regularly undertaken. These sessions are not *ad hoc*; they need careful planning and must have an agenda. A reflexivity session focuses on 'how' things are done. These sessions are about improving how the team works together and how team members go about doing whatever it is that they do. In essence, it is about innovating the way in which the team works. It is the intentional introduction, adaptation and application of ideas and procedures that are new to the team and which are designed to improve its effectiveness. One could consider reflexivity as a proxy for good communication and it is definitely a prerequisite for psychological safety. The higher the demands in terms of workload, the higher the demand for new and improved ways of working. Without taking time out on a regular basis, the team cannot expect to innovate and drive its effectiveness. Teams that do not communicate well suffer considerably more when overloaded or constantly dealing with high workload demands. High workloads block innovation, but this can be and is overcome by reflexivity.

As a process, reflexivity requires strong leadership and discipline. It requires a psychologically safe environment, while also helping to develop psychological safety as members are encouraged to say what is on their minds, no idea is considered ridiculous and equal air time is given to all members. It is essential to encourage quieter members to speak up in these sessions and express their views. This is about learning; it is about collective thought and respecting individual thought, and, as a process, fosters collective intelligence.

When leaders do not listen or reflect on how others and the team collectively perceive the situation, they are effectively shutting the members down. A leader in this situation can make themselves believe that the team members do not want to contribute and collaborate, when in fact the leader has prevented their engagement. Overachievers tend to want to command and coerce rather than collaborate and coach, and thereby stifle those around them. Team leaders need training in this reflexive process or, better still, need an external facilitator in the early stages to help establish working and robust practices.

Topic 3:
**Teams can only effectively change and innovate
through reflection, and this must be done through**

a process that is intentional and structured, where
time and space are made available for the team on a
regular basis. It is an imperative in these demanding
and challenging times. The time has come for organizations to make the coffee for these sessions. Organizations need to ensure that reflexive practice is an
established and recognized process for all teams with
the same importance attached to it as is attached to
performance management and other people practices.
It makes such sense and, for relatively small invest-
ments in time, the returns are exponential.

Team-based assessment

The winds of change are definitely blowing and no more so than
in the arena of people assessment. Performance appraisal (PA) at
long last has been recognized for the nonsense that it is and is
rapidly being abandoned.

The Institute for Corporate Productivity (I4CP) stated in 2016
that of 244 companies surveyed in the USA, 67% were rethinking
their performance management practices.[20]

The dreaded annual review, where an employee is 'appraised'
or 'evaluated' based on their individual performance in achieving
a set of goals over the previous 12 months, may soon be a thing
of the past.

In April 2015, *Harvard Business Review* devoted a ten-page
spread (titled "Reinventing Performance Management") to Deloitte's
new and *avant-garde* approach to performance management.[21]

Even GE, the originator of 'forced ranking' and the performance rating 'bell curve', has begun to overhaul its approach to
PA and to experiment with new ways of managing and reviewing
performance.

That these large organizations are dropping PA might suggest a
breakthrough in how they are dealing with the performance of their
employees. However, while this move might be a breakthrough

in management practice, it is by no means a breakthrough in management thinking. Where we go next is not yet clear.

This dramatic change in management practice has, however, raised the question of team-based assessment. Millennials and the gig economy are factors in driving a change in assessment means. Real time, little and often is what is now required. The 'rise of teams' and the new organization are creating an imperative for team-based assessment, integrated with individual assessment. In fact, the search for such a measurement can be described as the 'El Dorado' of assessment. It never ceases to amaze me how little team measurement is practised in organizations and how very few organizations can identify why one team seems to outperform another. As stated previously, very few teams are high performing. It is estimated that only 10% can truly be deemed high performing and a frightening 40% are dysfunctional, detrimental to the staff experience and should be disbanded or, at the very least, seriously reconfigured. The balance of 50% can at best be described as performing marginally and never producing more than incremental results.[22] With 90% of output happening through teams, organizations must recognize the absolute imperative of team assessment and measurement.

In every organization there will be teams that are clearly successful and those that struggle. These examples need to be explored to understand which characteristics and dynamics that surround them enable their success and/or failure. This process can lead to the development of a set of guiding principles for all teams in the organization to adopt, such as the development of the team mission and values, team operating principles, team planning and evaluation, and team processes. It will also facilitate the understanding of team leadership behaviours that support teams for success in the organization.

Team-based assessment requires a broader strategy, which for me is the development of a CTS. As with any strategy, the expected outcome of a CTS must be measurable and quantifiable. Early in the process of developing a CTS, the organization must determine which metrics will be used to measure the impact of their strategy. This measurement, or set of measurements, will be determined by the objectives set for the strategy. As part of this process, it is advisable for a structured team assessment tool to be deployed with all teams on a regular basis. The tool must allow for comparisons that demonstrate the progress of the team. This can then be correlated with a wide range of organizational metrics, as indicated in **Table 4**.

Table 4.
Suggested measurements for a CTS

Strategy objective	Measurement	Impact
Financial performance	Key financial indicators	Financial and productivity
Cost savings	Targeted cost reductions	Financial and productivity
Absenteeism	Specified reduction	Financial and productivity
Attrition/retention	Specified level	Financial and productivity
Performance management	Targeted % completed on time, real-time goal setting, increased individual and team goal attainment	Morale, motivation and productivity
Customer satisfaction	Specified level	Financial and customer retention
Cross-functional cooperation	Employee survey, focus groups or bespoke survey	Financial, productivity, morale and motivation
Training validation	Improvement in team scores on a recognized assessment or any of the above	Financial, training ROI and productivity

The introduction of a robust team assessment tool will also enable the understanding of an additional range of informative statistics, greatly supporting the organization's and team's drive to perform effectively. Typically such statistics may include:

- Company-specific norm data: This creates a continuing upward pressure on team performance as teams operating below the company norm cannot reject the statistic. It is far more powerful than market norm data, which can be rejected by a given team. This has the effect of serving to push the norm upwards.
- Optimal team size: By correlating any given metric (in this instance, often financial performance) with a team assessment tool, optimal team size can be established, which will have an impact on recruitment, retention, talent management, etc.
- Training validation: Mapping training success criteria to an instrument will facilitate the understanding of training impact and ultimately lead to an understanding of ROI.
- Leadership profiling: The most effective leaders for a given organization can be identified based on a robust team assessment instrument. This has a major impact for leadership training and development programmes and their design, recruitment and talent management.
- Training needs analysis: Integrating a team assessment tool into a strategy enhances the accuracy of training needs analysis for both team leaders and team members.

This not an exhaustive list but indicates what is possible with both a comprehensive CTS and a robust team tool.

Topic 4:

There are many factors driving the need for a change in assessment methods. Giggers, millennials, the rise of teams, the new organization and the demise of performance appraisal are all an imperative for team assessment as opposed to individual assessment. Around 90% of output is through teams and 40% of teams are dysfunctional. If ever there was a 'wake up and smell the coffee' moment, this is it.

Diversity and inclusion

In the multicultural and multi-ethnic societies in which we live and work, diversity and inclusion (D&I) has risen to the top of the agenda for many organizations. There has been, and continues to be, an ongoing stream of research confirming the impact and benefits of D&I. According to the Society for Human Resource Management, the US representative professional body for HR practitioners, 55% of companies are big promoters of D&I and 42% of D&I programmes are advocated by CEOs and C-level suites.[23] There is now an acceptance that those organizations with effective D&I strategies will outperform their competitors in terms of returns on equity and earnings before interest and tax (EBIT). Diverse and inclusive organizations are more innovative, generate a superior employer brand image and, in doing so, attract and retain talent more effectively, and appeal to a wider customer and supplier base.

With the compelling case for D&I, and the recognition of its importance by organizations, one would expect more headway to have been made based on the evidence. Yet, we still have under representation of women in management and on boards. We still have a substantial gender pay gap and, distressingly, we still have senior leadership teams unrepresentative of the organizations they lead. We still have boards and senior teams that are predominantly made up of middle-aged white males. Women account for only 20% of C-level suite members globally.[24] So much for true diversity.

Diversity and inclusion are mostly spoken about as the same concept. However, they are two very different issues and the failure to consider them separately is perhaps the reason we have not made the progress we should. Organizations, in my view, are more focused on diversity at the expense of inclusion. You need equal focus on both to derive the benefits.

By inclusion I mean the bringing together and harnessing of a diverse workforce in a way that is beneficial to both the individual and the organization. Inclusion is what enacts diversity, building a culture of involvement, respect and connection for employees, regardless of their diverse characteristics or level in the organization. It is seeking out and enabling those different perspectives, ideas and backgrounds to drive innovation and business value. What better way is there to deliver this inclusion than through a team-based culture and a CTS that delivers the new organization and the network of teams?

The benefits of D&I are as applicable to the team as they are to the overall organization. A team in every way is a mini organization and an organization is ultimately a network of teams. Inclusion is best delivered at the team level. In overall organizational terms, delivering inclusion through a comprehensive CTS is a very effective means of realizing this element of a D&I strategy.

Millennials, who by 2025 will represent 75% of the workforce,[5] view D&I very differently to baby boomers and Gen Xers. For the millennial, diversity is a given and their focus is on inclusion in a supportive, collaborative environment that values open participation from those with differing ideas, perspectives and attitudes, in a way that adds value to the business. The millennial does not believe that they should downplay their differences and personalities to get ahead. They want acceptance of their thoughts and opinions, but are not prepared to park their identities at the organization's door, believing strongly that these very differences are what create value, impact and outcomes.

Older generations, on the other hand, view D&I primarily through a diversity lens and see it as mainly to do with fairness and equity, regardless of gender, race, religion, ethnicity and sexual orientation. For them it is a moral and legal obligation – the right thing to do – whether or not it benefits the business.

The older generations are the ones who brought D&I to the table, but they are now holding back the development of D&I. Organizations need to take note and change their strategies or, at the very least, create an equal focus on the issues of inclusion along with diversity. By 2025, millennials will have taken over and they will drive the change.[5] The organization that gets in now will get ahead of the pack in terms of the benefits to be accrued.

Effective teams that embrace diversity, different sensibilities and areas of expertise, and are willing to collaborate and challenge each other to reach a common goal that will deliver results that are better thought through, more effective and more creative. This is a team that enjoys psychological safety, one of the prerequisites for an effective team. As a team they offer more potential solutions in challenging each other and see this as a means to the delivery of more rounded outcomes for the team, the organization and ultimately the end user of their output, be that a customer or internal client.

Diversity resists conformity and, in doing so, creates more conflict. Equally, an effective team also resists conformity, allowing all views to be expressed, and it is this conflict that drives innovation. There is nothing wrong with conflict; only with the manner in which we manage it. Effective teams encourage disagreement and diverse teams have it built in. Effective teams seek out disagreement and differences, and use them to identify common denominators that can widen the appeal of a service, product or outcome to a broader user base.

In many respects, when it comes to inclusion, we are talking about common decency, respect, acceptance, listening, valuing individuals, engagement, participation and basic good human relations. It does not matter if the lens is one of diversity or effective teamwork, the result is the same. Effective teams recognize that different opinions and perspectives exist, and see this as an advantage to be maximized. These teams are simply better in every respect than teams who do not.

For the organization of today and tomorrow – delivering inclusion as the enabler of diversity – there is a need to focus on teamwork and, more precisely, view the imperative of teams, teamwork and CTS as key elements of any D&I strategy.

Maybe it is time to expand the brief of all D&I leaders and functions to include responsibility for delivery of the team-based culture.

Topic 5:

D&I is a major focus for organizations today. Millennials perceive the concept differently to older generations and have a keener focus on inclusion through teamwork. The strategies that brought D&I to the table in the first place are becoming stale due to an overemphasis on the diversity element. Organizations must wake up and recognize the different coffees and give inclusion equal prominence on the menu. Delivering a CTS and a team-based culture based on a network of teams is a key platform for a truly inclusive workplace.

Morale and motivation in teams

Not that old chestnut again – how could morale and motivation be a hot topic? Nevertheless, I am bringing it back to the table for discussion. Along with the myths of teams (Chapter 2), this is a subject area that causes me serious grief.

In practically every team facilitation session I deliver, the issue of morale and motivation of either the employee body or the team emerges as a topic of conversation. The lack of understanding and agreement that exists around these two important concepts never ceases to amaze me.

Morale and motivation are concepts that are very poorly understood in general and yet they are perceived as critically important in an employee/workforce sense. In fact, many people will struggle to tell you the source of their own morale and motivation.

This lack of agreed understanding and definition has critical implications for any group attempting to address these issues. As one observes such a group in discussion, there is much head nodding and apparent agreement as various strategies to address the topics are discussed. Invariably a decision for action will be reached. This is where the problem emerges. As the group leave with a decision for action, the expectation of each member is entirely different and is based on their individual understanding of the concepts. The lack of clear definition within the group can mean that the actions determined for dealing with an issue of motivation are more ideally suited to issues of morale and, of course, the converse can also be true. The net outcome is a less than successful result, with the group wondering what went wrong and feeling that the target team must be at fault somehow.

For any organization or team, there must be an agreement as to what each term means. What does morale mean? What does motivation mean? In reaching these definitions it must be recognized that morale and motivation are two very separate issues, dealt with by very separate means, and they are not synonyms of each other. It must be understood that it is possible to have morale without motivation, but never motivation without morale.

It must be understood and agreed that morale and motivation cannot be 'done' to others. One can create the conditions where an individual will experience morale and may therefore exercise motivation, but both are ultimately personal. They are different for everyone. They are life-stage dependent, and relative to ambition and the philosophy of working to live or living to work. Not everyone's satisfaction is derived from their work. Work can be a means to other ends.

Here are my definitions of both concepts.

Morale

Morale is the mental and emotional condition (such as enthusiasm, confidence or loyalty) of an individual or group with regard to the function or tasks at hand. It is a common sense of purpose with respect to a group.

Morale can also be referred to as *esprit de corps* (the most appropriate synonym) – the level of individual psychological wellbeing based on such factors as a sense of purpose and confidence in the future. *Esprit de corps* embodies a sense of wanting to belong for the now.

Morale is an experiential condition. Based on the conditions surrounding them, a group or individual will experience good, average or poor morale. It is a state of mind.

The key terms and words one needs to focus upon from this definition shown in **Figure 2.**

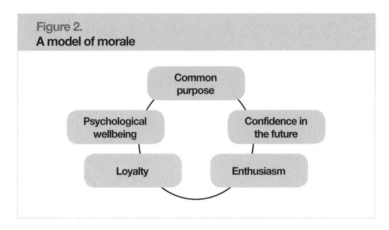

Figure 2.
A model of morale

From a team leader's perspective, the practical implications of this definition, and where to focus one's effort in terms of creating the conditions for morale to be experienced by the team, are summarized in **Table 5.**

Table 5.
Key areas of focus for morale

Key concept	Focus areas	Detail
Common purpose	• Goals	• Team mission, individual goals and understanding that the collective achievement of goals delivers the mission
Confidence in the future	• Goals • Planning	• Ensure goals are relatable, achievable, interesting and challenging • Clear plans that tell the team where to go and when they will get there
Enthusiasm	• Communication • Composition	• Continuous communication with no vacuums • Understand skill base, coach, and listen to and encourage all ideas
Loyalty	• Conflict • Organization	• Develop rules of engagement • Maximize skills by astute allocation of responsibilities; give time to organizing your resources effectively
Psychological wellbeing	• All of the above	• Adopt the inverted hierarchy

Motivation

Defining motivation is far more difficult than defining morale. Motivation is a more complex issue due to the number of theories that abound. One's preferred theory determines one's understanding of the subject and often the approach to dealing with the issues of motivation.

By my most recent calculations, I estimate there to be more than 100 theories of motivation in circulation. Maslow, Hertzberg, McClelland and McGregor (not necessarily in that order) are the most readily quoted when it comes to a discussion of motivation. In most instances, while the theories are known, they are seldom understood in a meaningful manner in terms of teams. To arrive at a useful way of doing something about motivation for teams, we must first undertake a short overview of the historical emergence of motivation theory from its inception to the present day.

Motivation comes from the Latin word *'movere'* meaning 'movement'. It was originally a philosophical concept and, as a subject of study, migrated to psychology in the mid-19th century. Psychology is today defined as the scientific study of behaviour and mental processes.

The original philosophical understanding of motivation was based on hedonism, in that instinct, drive and habit resulting from the past became the basis for understanding. According to this view, we repeat what is pleasurable and reject anything that is unpleasant. This resulted in a set of theories collectively referred to as 'reinforcement theories'.

In the 1950s and 1960s, the acknowledgement of social influences and the complexity of people led to the emergence of the content theories. Also referred to as 'needs' theories, these included Maslow (Hierarchy of Needs), McClelland (Simultaneous and Competing Needs), Herzberg (Two Factor Theory – Hygiene Factors and Motivators), McGregor (Theory Y and Theory X) and many more. The principal aim of these theories was to identify the factors associated with motivation.

The late 1960s and early 1970s saw the emergence of process theories on motivation, central to which were the cognitive theories. These new conceptualizations of motivation are more directly relatable to the workplace and view motivation from a dynamic perspective, looking at causal relationships across time and events as they relate to human nature in the workplace.

So, which do we use to understand motivation and ultimately apply in the working environment?

There is no easy answer to this question. I believe that a combination of the needs theories with the cognitive theories best helps us to understand motivation in the workplace. Specifically, I refer to the theories of Maslow (Hierarchy of Needs), Herzberg (Two Factor Theory – Hygiene and Motivators) and McGregor (Theory X Theory Y) from the needs school, and Vroom (Expectancy Theory) and Latham and Lock (Goal Setting Theory) from the cognitive school.

In practical terms, what can a team leader do to create the conditions where team members will exercise motivation? At the outset I stated that motivation is not possible without morale. The first order of business for a team leader in terms of motivation is to address the issues of morale as previously described. They are intrinsically linked.

With morale being addressed, I believe that there are areas a leader can focus on to create the conditions where motivation has every chance of being exercised by team members (see **Table 6**).

Table 6.
Key areas of focus for motivation

Key concept	Focus areas	Detail
Leadership	• Disposition • The inverted hierarchy	• Theory Y disposition – a belief that people are naturally positive in their attitudes • As a leader, you are there to support and not be supported
Participation	• Flexible leadership style • Psychological safety	• Deliver appropriate style to each team member based on their needs; one style does not fit all • Deliver on the issues of psychological safety – build an open and honest environment
Roles	• Consistency	• Schedule and provide complete regular clarifications on role and goal clarity
Commitment	• Consistency	• Cannot be addressed directly • Ensure the issues of morale are addressed • Dependent on the other five areas
Evaluation	• Trust and reliability	• Ensure, in consultation with team, appropriate evaluation methods for tasks and goals • Commit to regular reflective time for the team to consider the *modus operandi*
Recognition	• Feedback – individual and team based	• Complete regular feedback with individuals – informal rather than formal • Complete regular team feedback on overall performance • Support weaker performers early in a cycle • Remember the inverted hierarchy

Topic 6:

Morale is experienced whereas motivation is exercised – neither can be done to anyone. Leaders at all levels need to wake up and recognize that morale and motivation are very different, like coffee and tea. They are similar, aimed at a common outcome, but made very differently. In both cases, organizations can only create the conditions for them to arise. After that, it is up to the individual to respond.

Chapter 4.

The imperative of a team effectiveness model

> **Effectiveness**
> *The ability to be successful and produce the intended results.*
> *For the team, success is achieving the results, but effectiveness is*
> *about capability for success.*

A CTS is about building the capability of teams throughout the organization, developing them to be effective and drive organizational success. There must be a starting point in this process and for me this is the adoption of an appropriate team model for effectiveness. There are literally hundreds of models for team effectiveness. Just enter 'images for team effectiveness' into a web search bar and you will see what I mean. So, how does one select a model?

Determining a model

The determination of a model is based on a number of factors. The model must be easily understood by all and it must be chosen by the organization for team leaders and team members in the first instance, not for the elite organizational development or HR practitioner. Yes, it must be a verifiable model and it must have established reliability that it does what it says it does. However, I recommend staying away from overly complex models; a model must be usable by the team on an ongoing basis in a self-managed process if it is to be deployed across the organization. Allowing for some briefing and upskilling, each team should be able to deploy the model and methodology without ongoing support. The key to a successful and useful model and methodology is in its capacity for continued, repeated and regular use without creating a major imposition on time. Depending on the availability of an 'expert' severely limits the deployment of any approach. A successful CTS will aim for self-sufficiency and self-management for teams and leaders in terms of driving their effectiveness. If, alongside these factors, organizations encourage teams to regularly take the time to consider 'how' they do things, there will be an overall improvement in team effectiveness and impact for the bottom line.

An additional key consideration in choosing a model is the availability of an assessment tool that enables the team to continually assess their challenges against the model. Most importantly, the suitability of the tool to generate assessment-to-assessment comparisons is paramount. This will provide the team with an ongoing barometer to indicate its progress and the impact of its actions based on the tool's output. The tool should have the capacity to be correlated with other key business metrics and allow the organization to create benchmarks for successful and/or failing teams. The language of the model and tool should be recognizable to as wide a population as possible and not be biased towards one type of team versus another – for example they should not use very technical, medical, production or sales-oriented language.

Issue 1:

Choose a model carefully. There are many to choose from. Whatever you pick will be with you for a long time and your chosen model is the basis for all else in driving team effectiveness. It is a big menu and as confusing as any coffee menu – from lattes to americanos to mochas to iced coffee, with syrup, cream or marshmallows – it is never ending! They are all coffee and yet very different at the same time. So are all the models out there.

Distinguishing between behavioural and effectiveness measures

Many organizations will be familiar with behavioural-based instruments, such as Belbin,[25] Insights,[26] Myers Briggs,[27] DISC,[28] True Colors,[29] NEO Birkman,[30] Hogan,[31] OPQ[32] and so on.

These instruments are based on the psychology of behaviour in the team and I am all in favour of their use. They are powerful tools and provide very valuable information to a team. They do, however, tend to be complex, requiring training and accreditation for their use and implementation. They do not, for the most part, allow for assessment comparisons that track team progression and do not easily lend themselves to correlation with other key business metrics. Behavioural assessments have a focus on the individual and how the collective makes up the team, not on the team as an intact unit. Where these assessments use only self-perception, they may not yield the insights and learnings that are generated when an individual's colleagues provide feedback.

I tend to distinguish between behavioural assessment instruments focused on the individual and those that measure team effectiveness more holistically. Behavioural characteristics can be understood, and the team can organize to maximize the impact of their combined characteristics, but they cannot be substantially changed. We are what we are. Team effectiveness, in terms of aspects such as goals and role clarity, can be controlled by the team and changed to improve overall team effectiveness. In the ideal world, a team will deploy a team effectiveness model regularly, say quarterly, and a behavioural-based assessment as an initial benchmark of behavioural competencies and as demanded by team composition changes.

Issue 2:

Choosing an assessment instrument must be done with the end game in mind. What are you trying to achieve? What is the objective? To what extent do you want to integrate the model with other metrics and key business processes? Is your choice a one-off for a single team or is it for all teams? It is a bit like deciding between decaffeinated and caffeinated. They taste the same, kind of, but one sure has a bigger kick.

Introducing the TDP model

Working globally with teams for many years, my colleagues and I at The ODD Company[33] have developed an effectiveness model, assessment tool and methodology for teams to drive performance. In doing so we created a process that is easy to use, quick to apply, self-serve, results-oriented, action-focused, operationally driven and capable of integrating with key business methods and metrics. The Team Diagnostic Profiler© model (TDP)[33] came to fruition over a number of years. It is a model of team effectiveness but also an integrated methodology to support teams. TDP is comprised of the model, an assessment tool and a comprehensive but easy-to-follow analysis process for the team. The validation and reliability studies for TDP were completed on 600 teams and 3,000 individuals.

Since teams themselves hold the answers in terms of what is best for them and what will work best in their situation, a model that improves effectiveness is not one that tells teams what to do. It will not say if you do x then y is guaranteed. Correctly implemented, it is an approach that respects the team's integrity and recognizes that, given time and opportunity to reflect, a team can and will enhance their own effectiveness. What is required is a robust structure for the team to have the conversation and reflect on effectiveness measures that work for them.

I am not suggesting TDP is the best or only model. However, it is a model and methodology that can form the basis for an effective CTS and that has, in that regard, some additional utility compared to others. It has been developed with the team leader and team members in mind.

TDP is based on the principle that all teams hold the answers to their own effectiveness but need dedicated time to be reflective and talk about themselves and how they work together. The TDP assessment instrument and methodology are designed to create the agenda for a structured team discussion using data derived from the team members. Repeated use on a regular basis allows the team to track the impact of their improvement actions through the assessment-to-assessment comparison reporting function.

TDP is focused on the issues of team effectiveness and not the behavioural composition of the team in terms of member personalities. Again, I recognize the value of behavioural profiling but chose, in developing the model, to focus on the issues that a team can manage and change to drive their effectiveness. In doing so, the team can ultimately deliver the conditions of a safe psychological environment where all team members can, without fear, ask any question, admit to weaknesses, offer ideas and challenge the status quo. TDP ultimately creates the learning environment that the team needs to innovate and drive improvement that leads to increased effectiveness.

TDP is about all the teams in an organization and not just the 'problem' team.

By using familiar language together with an analysis methodology and assessment tool that are easy to assimilate, TDP is self-serve for the team leader and does not require ongoing 'expert' facilitation. Once deployed, TDP becomes an embedded process for the team and is implemented regularly without placing unreasonable time demands on the team. It is easily accommodated within a team's ongoing schedule.

Figure 3 denotes the key constituents of the model in six factors, each of which has two criteria. Team members respond to 12 polarized items on a 7-point scale (see **Table 7**), which generates a report on the status of the team in terms of the members' perceptions. Following the completion of the assessment, the team conducts a structured analysis of the output to determine where its challenges lie in terms of effectiveness and plan its actions to improve. It is an action learning cycle. There is no ideal state, only what the team considers effective for them.

Figure 3.
The TDP model © The ODD Company

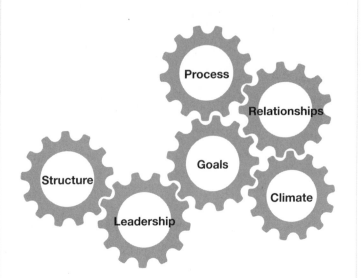

Goals
Team members need to be clear about the goals of the team and
how their role contributes to its achievement.

Leadership
Leadership behaviour has to help the team achieve its goals and
encourage participation.

Relationships
Effective teams require good communications and trust
between members.

Process
There have to be appropriate planning and evaluation techniques
to build an organic team.

Climate
Conflict has to be managed and recognition provided for different levels
of performance to generate a positive climate.

Structure
Team members must be organized appropriately and have the skills
to achieve their goals.

Table 7 displays the items that team members are required to respond to. The key to a TDP output is not in the responses delivered but in the structured discussion that follows.

Table 7.
TDP item bank © The ODD Company

Factor	Criteria	Negative pole	Positive pole
Goals	Goal clarity	The goals of this team are unclear to me	The goals of this team are clear to me
	Role clarity	I am unclear about how my role in this team contributes to goals	I am clear about how my role in this team contributes to goals
Leadership	Behaviour	Leadership behaviour in this team does not help us towards our goals	Leadership behaviour in this team does help us towards our goals
	Participation	Leadership behaviour in this team does not actively encourage participation	Leadership behaviour in this team actively encourages participation
Relationships	Commitment	It is difficult to rely on other team members	Team members can always be relied upon
	Communication	Team members are not honest in their communication	Team members are honest in their communication
Process	Planning	We do not use any appropriate planning techniques for our team tasks	We use appropriate planning techniques for our team tasks
	Evaluation	We do not use any appropriate evaluation techniques for our team tasks	We use appropriate evaluation techniques for our team tasks
Climate	Recognition	This team does not distinguish between good, average and poor performance among members	This team does distinguish between good, average and poor performance among members
	Conflict	When conflict arises within this team we do not deal with it effectively	When conflict arises within this team we deal with it effectively
Structure	Composition	This team does not have the correct skill sets to achieve our goals	This team does have the correct skill sets to achieve our goals
	Organization	The way we are organized in this team is inappropriate to our goals	The way we are organized in this team is appropriate to our goals

The TDP items are presented to respondents randomly, one at a time, in the following format:

Point 1 represents the negative pole and point 7 the positive pole.

Let's consider goal clarity as an example. No matter the result of a team's response to this item, there is a conversation required and the questions the team must address are: What have we got? Why have we got it? and What are we going to do about it? If we assume that the team members have all responded with a 7 on the scale for goal clarity, indicating they are all clear on the goals, then the "What have we got?" question, when applied to the apparent clarity in goals, leads to an interesting discussion. What is it we are clear on? What are the goals of the team? It will often become apparent that, while the team members claim clarity, they are all 'clear' on different things. In effect, there is no team goal clarity. This leads to the next question: "Why have we got it?" Why are we seeing things differently? Why are we this way? Why do we not have agreed goals despite apparent clarity? There can be many reasons for such a scenario but, bottom line, the team is not aligned and this will have a major impact on effectiveness. The final question becomes obvious: "What are we going to do about it?" This leads to an action plan, the impact of which is assessed following the next implementation of TDP. Simple but powerful.

This process is repeated until each of the 12 criteria have been discussed. The key is for the team to identify their priorities in terms of their *modus operandi* and to find the most important impediment to effective teamwork, and in addressing that see what other areas are impacted. At each subsequent session, the team pick up on their agreed actions from the previous session and their implementation in the intervening period, assess the impact and move on to the next challenges identified by TDP and their responses.

Issue 3:
**TDP is a model, an assessment tool and
a methodology, designed to support the team leader's
self-management of the process. Simple but powerful –
probably the best and easiest instant coffee in the
world to make, with a great flavour.**

Additional benefits of a model-based approach

The TDP model can be directly linked to morale and motivation and these links are outlined in **Table 8**. It might be useful to revisit the focus areas I identified in Chapter 3 in considering the links below. Creating links such as these, in effect, brings a practical application and means to management theory. It brings theory alive and provides leaders and teams with an objective and real means of addressing such concepts.

Table 8.
Linking morale and motivation to the TDP model

TDP factor	TDP criteria	Issue of morale	Issue of motivation
Goals	Goal clarity	√	
	Role clarity		√
Leadership	Behaviour		√
	Participation		√
Relationships	Commitment		√
	Communication	√	
Process	Planning	√	
	Evaluation		√
Climate	Recognition		√
	Conflict	√	
Structure	Composition	√	
	Organization	√	

Remember that morale is experienced and motivation is exercised. These are distinct personal issues for the individual. They are dependent on the conditions created in the team. The leader and the team can create the conditions where there is every chance that members will experience positive morale and exercise motivation, but you cannot 'do' morale and motivation to people. Linking these concepts to a model such as TDP gives a leader and team a clear agenda for the areas they need to focus on to create the necessary conditions. It makes the intangible and nebulous clear, tangible and actionable.

There are many additional benefits to a model-based approach, particularly that it is embedded in a CTS, is obligatory for all teams, is designed to be self-serving for team leaders and does not always require an 'expert'.

Having a model as a base or platform begins a process of standardizing the language of teams across the organization. A common model and tool opens up the possibilities for cross-team support, where team leaders can share ideas, skills and solutions, and even be in a position to facilitate feedback sessions for each other. This type of scenario can have a major impact on the development of a network of teams – the newly sought organizational structure. Making team reflection an obligation supports the idea of an inclusive culture, ensuring that leaders and teams determine how they should work and agree their priorities together. This has an immediate effect on communication and engagement.

Organizations need to identify the team effectiveness model that best suits them. There are so many to choose from. They can all serve similar purposes when integrated into an effective CTS. Some are more useful than others, while some are purely academic in nature and not very helpful from a team leader's and team member's perspective. Go for simplicity as opposed to complexity. You will get better and more consistent results in the short, medium and long term. Make sure the model chosen is right for your organization and that it has been developed for use as described in this chapter.

In Chapters 9 to 14, I will take each of the factors of TDP, and their respective criteria, and examine them in detail in terms of their meaning and content. I will also explain the approach a team may take to improve their effectiveness in each area.

Issue 4:

A model for teamwork is a critical element of any organization that wishes to drive team development with consistency and it can impact, integrate with and enhance many aspects of culture. It is the coffee bean, the basis on which a variety of coffee drinks can be prepared. Without the bean, there is no coffee; without the team effectiveness model, there is nothing to base a CTS or team development initiative upon.

Part 2.

What kind of coffee do we have anyway?

Not all teams are the same and not all teams can be resourced, developed and led in the same manner. There are similarities between teams and in effect all teams are derivatives of the original traditional intact team.

Part 2 of this book focuses on what I consider to be the four basic team types we have today – the traditional intact team, the project team, the virtual team and the teaming work group. Many will argue that I have excluded important team types from my analysis. However, I contend that the four presented here are sound platforms in terms of any and all team types. The characteristics, the challenges and the nature of the teams presented effectively describe the issues to a greater or lesser extent for all teams. The four basic team types that will be considered in the next four chapters are outlined in **Figure 4**.

This is the 'determining the type of coffee bean' part of the book. To decide the best way to make your coffee, you must first understand what kind of bean you have. Then you can decide whether it should be filtered, percolated, pour-over dripped, plunged or vacuum syphoned. Each method produces coffee but with a different means and different tastes. So it is with teams. Teams are all about collaborative working but must be assembled, led, resourced and understood as appropriate to their nature.

Figure 4.
The four basic team types

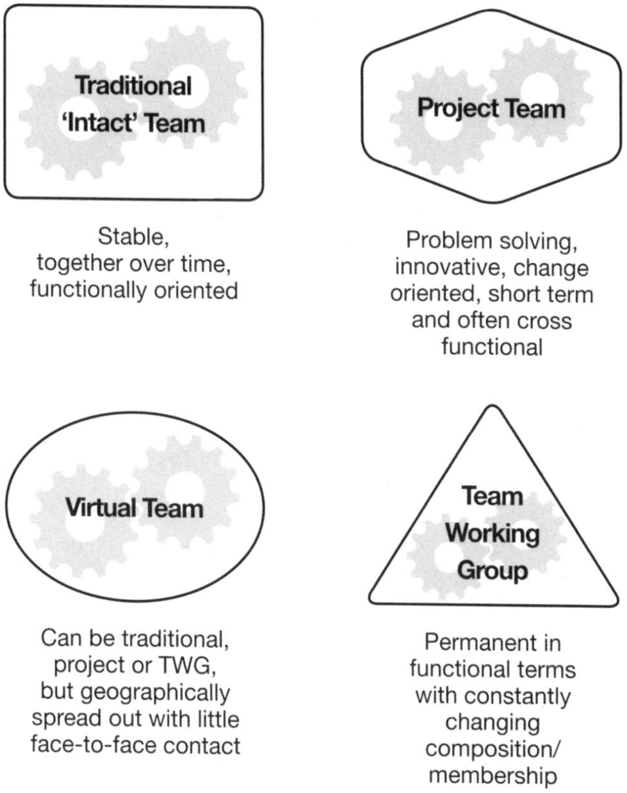

Traditional 'Intact' Team

Stable,
together over time,
functionally oriented

Project Team

Problem solving,
innovative, change
oriented, short term
and often cross
functional

Virtual Team

Can be traditional,
project or TWG,
but geographically
spread out with little
face-to-face contact

Team Working Group

Permanent in
functional terms
with constantly
changing
composition/
membership

Chapter 5.

The traditional team

Tradition

Long-established, adhering to past practices or established conventions. Comes from the Latin noun traditio, *from the verb* tradere — *to transmit, to hand over, to give for safekeeping.*

I need to reiterate what I mean by a team. As outlined in the Introduction, it is a group of people, normally fewer than ten, that need to work together to achieve a common goal, normally with a single leader and where there is a high degree of interdependence between the team members to achieve the goal or goals.

The traditional team is the team we are all most familiar with. Unfortunately, we have a tendency to refer to departments and entire functions as teams. Take HR as an example. In a large organization, there may be 50 or 100 people in the function. Within that there will be departments and within those again there will be teams. When I speak about a team, I am talking about this subset of a department, which, in turn, is a subset of the function. This applies to all functions, as in the finance function, the IT function, the production function or the sales function. In a small organization, these groupings may very well fit the criteria for a team in terms of size, while at the same time being an entire department and/or the entire function of the organization. Hence the confusion with the term in many instances. What starts out as a true team in terms of size, grows and expands into a department with multiple teams and finally into a function with multiple departments, but we still refer to it as 'the team'.

The traditional team is a functional team where specialists work together and share a common operational language. The leadership of this type of team is predetermined by the hierarchical structure of the organization and is often led by the most senior person in that team. The team is normally inherited by its leader and new members are recruited to the team based on their technical skills and not necessarily for their teaming attributes.

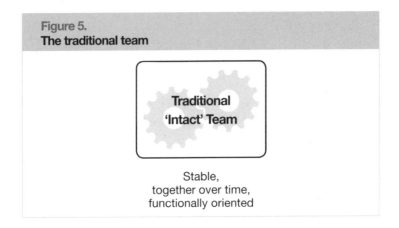

Figure 5.
The traditional team

Traditional 'Intact' Team

Stable,
together over time,
functionally oriented

The traditional team is relatively stable over time. It exists year to year, generally with a low rate of change in composition, with leavers replaced as required. The team is, for the most part, engaged in what are described as routine tasks – that is, tasks that are repeated continually, based on a team member's specialization. Occasionally, new projects or tasks are introduced that may involve a single member of the team, a few members of the team or the entire team. These new projects and tasks tend to relate to the introduction of a new method or new technology, or the integration of an expanded brief for the team. Once introduced, they become part of the routine.

The traditional team is the team that has been with us the longest in a work context. It emerged from the Industrial Revolution as mass production became a reality and the division of labour became a prerequisite for efficient manufacturing. It is a key characteristic of the functional bureaucracy. Throw the word 'bureaucracy' into the mix and people immediately begin to think ineffective, slow, cumbersome – it is a word that is seen in more of a negative than positive light. However, functional bureaucracies are very effective organizations. They have been with us for a long time and have, indeed, withstood the test of time – armies, religions and governments are all functional bureaucracies and they all do the job. They may be slow to change and adapt, but they are robust.

The strengths

The traditional team tends to be collocated and members work in close proximity to each other. This is, in fact, one of the major strengths of this team type. The proximity of the members to each other drives a number of advantages not available to other team types. Transactive memory (a transactive memory system is a mechanism through which groups collectively encode, store and retrieve knowledge)[34] happens for the traditional team day-to-day, as much through their informal communications as it does through their formal communications. Verbal clues, gestures and mannerisms all develop, which help to inform the team of the current situation, environment or even concerns of the individuals within the team as much as the team overall. Continuous face-to-face interactions encourage enhanced interpersonal relationships, developing a rapport within the group that improves effectiveness and efficiency. This has a beneficial impact on the psychological bond between team members. The bond is reinforced daily, making the team more robust in terms of its capacity to absorb smaller and more minor instances or misunderstandings, which can be detrimental to a team's performance. Traditional teams develop both transactive memory and a psychological bond intuitively in their day-to-day, face-to-face communication. The virtual team, the project team and the TWG need to create transactive memory artificially and consciously work at ensuring its availability and transmission.

The traditional team was developed on the basis of division of labour and this, in turn, delivers benefits for the team and organization. In this kind of team, specialists work together to provide support for in-depth competence, with many people talking the same operational language. It is also easier to attract specialization to this kind of team. Specialists tend to appreciate working with like-minded individuals who share their 'business speak' and are more likely to share their world views. This type of grouping also benefits from efficiency in terms of resources, as equipment and people are clustered centrally. Other team types drive a need for duplication of resources and come at a higher cost to the organization.

Equally, there is freedom to specialize while others do the coordination, providing opportunities for each team member to maximize what they do best. Management structures above the specialists take care of the broader concerns and issues, integrating specialized output into the organizational strategy and providing direction.

There is stability and security for team members in this type of team. The chain of command is clear, communication flows are delineated on the vertical axis, job roles are clear and centred on specialization, and the individual is recruited to the team based on their specialization. The stable and clear structure is a major contributor to a team member's sense of security and job purpose. Change in this team environment is comparably slower than in other team types and quick responses to change are not always essential. This further contributes to a sense of security and stability.

All in all, the traditional team is a practical, robust and stable approach to team delivery. Based on my experience and observations, traditional teams probably account for 60% of all teams in play today. It is a safe approach (in line with the definition of tradition provided), minimizes risk and is more supporting of team members than other team types.

The challenges

For all its strengths, the traditional team has many challenges that need to be understood and managed. As with any team, it cannot be assumed that it will effectively perform and maximize the identified benefits.

Since the leader is determined by seniority via the organizational hierarchy, it may be that the most appropriate team leader is not in place. Promotions tend to result from technical competence and not necessarily people management skills. As people skills are factored more and more into the equation these days, there is also an assumption that an individual who has reached a certain level in the hierarchy has the leadership skills required. Technical leadership and people management skills (as in performance management competence, people administrative skills) should not be confused with team leadership skills, which few of us have naturally. The former skills may help, but team leadership is a skill that needs to be developed. Poor or inappropriate leadership is a primary reason for a team becoming dysfunctional.

In many instances, the organization values the technical skills of the individual far more than their leadership skills. There is even a forgiving or excusing attitude adopted by the organization – "Joe's skill set is difficult to find. If we call him to task for his leadership approach he will leave and then where will we be?" Joe is allowed to happily continue and his belief that he is a great leader is further embellished by his high-performance rating. This dysfunctional behaviour, both by the organization in allowing it and by the leader in the way he acts, has major repercussions for performance and has a devastating effect on morale. This scenario is not uncommon. Technical skills are important, without question, but so are leadership skills and both are required to effectively lead a team. Ensuring that those charged with team leadership responsibilities are supported, educated and coached as leaders is, in my view, an absolute requirement.

People who share the same specialization and who operate functionally tend to perceive the world through their specific lens. The demands of their functional role conditions their perception of time and priorities, and, ultimately, their identification of problems and their subsequent solution. This is an element of the differentiation and integration theory made famous by Lawrence and Lorsch (1967).[35] It may be dated now, but it remains a brilliant piece of research that explains not only why we have conflict in organizations, but also how we inadvertently build it in when designing organizations.

Differentiation and integration theory tells us people involved in production perceive the world in minutes and hours. Any problem they encounter requires an immediate fix or production is halted. Sales, on the other hand, tend to think in months and quarters, with solutions to problems required in that time -frame. R&D will address a problem in terms of years. For them, the solution lies in the next release of a product or a new system in development. Each can perceive themselves to be the most important element. Sales believe they are keeping everyone in a job, production believe that without them sales would have nothing to sell and R&D see themselves protecting the long-term security of the business. The net result is that intergroup conflict is more predictable among traditional teams. There is nothing wrong with these differing time perceptions and, in fact, the organization needs them, but they must be understood and managed. Time perception will always be a challenge for the traditional team in the context of the overall organization. Leaders need to be very aware of this phenomenon and have a continuous focus on the conflict issues that it can drive, particularly between teams. Remember, every team has to succeed for the organization to succeed and differing time perceptions are natural and important. To succeed, teams must interact with others at some point, however cursory or interdependent that interaction is. Inter-team conflict can have a major impact on overall organizational performance.

Traditional work teams are part of a whole hierarchy and its functional bureaucracy. The decision-making process is slower, as there is a need for the information to go up the line. This can result in 'bottlenecking' and decisions piling up at the top. Nothing can be more frustrating for an individual employee than waiting, time and time again, for a decision to come down. For them it is critical, whereas for those making the decision it may not seem as important and can get pushed to the bottom of the pile. Time perceptions yet again. Because traditional teams are vertically controlled, they are dependent on fewer and fewer leaders as decisions go up the chain. There is an inevitable slowing down of the process, precisely because there are fewer decision makers, with only so much time on their hands.

Few members of the traditional team understand the 'big picture' as they are focused on their own specialization. This is true not only of the overall organizational picture but often also of the team's overall big picture and can create a need for leaders to continually reinforce how each team member and the overall team contribute to the whole. This failure to understand or be aware of the overall can and does lead to priorities being misconstrued. It enhances conflict between teams and team members, as each perceives the world through their own particular lens.

Traditional team members become focused (correctly so) on routine tasks and can find it difficult to shift direction quickly when required. Routine can lead to complacency, and continuous repetition and time pressure often prevent the team from considering their *modus operandi*. Innovation can be hampered in this situation. Team meetings are invariably about operational issues, with individual team members reporting to the leader on their area of expertise. Indeed, the team meeting can appear to the outsider as a series of one-to-ones with an audience. Innovation can be lost in the traditional team as a common phrase often overheard is, "We have always done it like this". This is not out of place in the traditional team as, by definition, the team adheres to past practices and established conventions.

The imperatives

Because traditional teams are so common and delineated by functional specialization, they are often overlooked in terms of their team development needs. Individual skills development takes place but, again, seldom in the context of the overall team requirements or in the context of an overall organizational team strategy. To maximize the potential of this type of team, and address its challenges, the organization and the leader must commit time and effort. While this can be done team by team with each team treated in isolation, it is more effective when any initiative taken is based on an integrated team strategy for the organization – a CTS.

Organizations must ensure that leaders of this type of team are supported to develop their team management and team facilitation skills as much as their general management and leadership skills. This includes mission and goal development, role clarification, planning and evaluation methods, performance management and conflict management, to name a few. In reality, the development subject matter is similar for all team types, but it needs to be delivered with the team type in mind. The leadership skills required for traditional teams are different from those of other teams. As indicated previously, the challenges must be addressed for the leader and the team in terms of a development initiative, tailored to the specific needs of the team type.

As with any team, goal clarity must never be considered a given and should be clarified regularly. The purpose of the team should also be clarified and constantly reviewed for its appropriateness in how it supports the overall organization. Critical in this process is to prevent the silo mentality that can develop around functional/traditional teams, leading to the purpose of the team becoming dominant in the minds of the team members at the expense of the overall organization. Rather than serving the organization, the team can become self-serving to the detriment of all. Leaders should ensure team members understand how they contribute to the overall picture, and also maintain the team's mindfulness of time perceptions and how they can distort priorities and drive unnecessary conflict.

Due to the stable nature of this team type, job roles are too often ignored and allowed to evolve without the required attention. All roles change with time. As an individual grows with experience in a role, they take on more, do things differently, drop tasks and take on others not in the original job description. It would be highly surprising if there were not some change in every role over 12 months. Attention to the definition of team roles is important, along with conducting regular reviews, and confirming and recording of pertinent changes. Check this out in your own organization. You will be surprised at what you find.

The traditional team must take time out to consider their own *modus operandi*, at the very least, on a quarterly basis. This is more about 'how' they do things rather than 'what' they do. This must be in addition to their operational meetings, where the 'what' they do is continually addressed. Making this happen, at least quarterly, ensures that the team has the opportunity to address innovation, which can be a major challenge for some traditional teams, due to the repetitious nature of their tasks and the complacency this repetition can imbue.

Through a CTS, the organization should develop a set of team standards that apply to all teams in the organization. For example, all teams should have a clear mission statement and goal clarification process, and should carry out a stakeholder analysis to ensure that their mission meets the different stakeholder needs, as the stakeholder needs can vary greatly for each team. Each team should develop operating principles and hold each other to account in terms of their implementation. They should also have a suitable planning and evaluation methodology for progress that is regularly deployed.

Traditional team leaders should be obliged to review their leadership style with their team in terms of its appropriateness relative to the team's stage of development or maturity. As a leader, just because you are appointed in the hierarchy to lead a traditional team, do not assume the stability of that appointment or, indeed, that the stable nature of the team means that there will not be substantive change happening on an ongoing basis. The issues of leadership behaviour and appropriateness cannot be ignored. The team members change, the leader changes, even the purpose of the team can change, and the smart leader will recognize this fact and adapt accordingly. The traditional team is constantly evolving; the members, though stable in composition, are also evolving, maturing and developing. The style of leadership must also evolve and develop and be appropriate to the needs of the team. This can only be done effectively in consultation with the team and I suggest that it should be done twice yearly as a minimum.

The complacency that can set in with the performance of
routine tasks, a characteristic of the traditional team, should be
constantly monitored. All teams must be encouraged to continually evaluate their performance, not just those teams that are
displaying issues or concerns.

In a final consideration, it must be noted that the traditional
team is comprised of individuals with specific job/organizational
roles. Some of their time is spent working on an individual basis.
Not every task and action is team based. However, more and
more, interdependency between roles to get the job done is a
reality. It is in the areas of task and role interdependency that the
application of team skills matters.

Practical, robust and stable, albeit slow to change,
the traditional team not only has value but also has
a place in organizations where routine and repetitive
tasks are a requirement. The traditional team is like
the Arabica coffee bean. Both are the original of the
species. Both still account for about 60% of their
kind, in terms of world consumption or deployment.
Original and best? Not always. Both have their limitations. The Arabica bean is susceptible to coffee
leaf rust (a nasty thing) while the traditional team,
because of its nature, can become dysfunctional due
to complacency (an equally nasty thing).

Chapter 6.

The project team

> **Project**
>
> *A piece of carefully planned work or an activity that is finished over a period of time and intended to achieve a particular purpose, with a beginning and an end, and, as such, is considered a closed dynamic system. It is bound by the constraints of calendar, costs and norms of quality, each of which can be determined and measured objectively along the project life cycle.*

Project teams have become increasingly common in many organizations and are now viewed as essential in reacting quickly, meeting changing customer needs, driving innovation and adapting continuously to the environment. There are organizations today that are structured entirely around project teams for client delivery. This type of organization creates a different culture and experience from the more traditional functional team-based organization, with a perceived faster pace, energy and momentum. This is not to suggest that this is a better form of organization.

At the macro level, environmental conditions influence the degree to which any organizational structure can be effective. Volatile environments, which provide uncertain or unreliable information, require less structure. This is typical in sectors such as technology, software and gaming, which are constantly facing rapid change. Conversely, stable environments, which provide reliable information, require more structure – such as professional services, hospitals and state organizations.

Environments driven by rapid technological discoveries and by the frequent and rapid introduction of innovative and improved processes are likely to be unforgiving of a procedurally bound functional bureaucracy. Such organizations would have difficulty interpreting uncertain environmental information, be slow to notice and respond to change, and be too inflexible to cope with or respond to changing conditions. Under these circumstances, their very survival would be in question, as more agile competitors would exploit

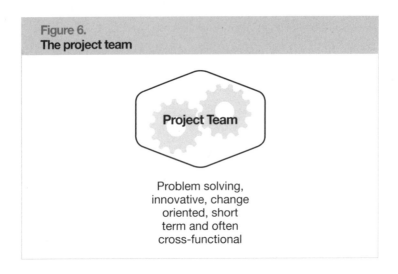

Figure 6.
The project team

Project Team

Problem solving,
innovative, change
oriented, short
term and often
cross-functional

the inappropriate fit. In contrast, in stable environments in which change is minimal and information is clear, the same functional bureaucratic characteristics might very well become valuable assets, offering those organizations a distinct competitive advantage. No one form is better than another. It is a matter of horses for courses.[35]

In a fast-moving environment, the project team comes into its own. It can be assembled and disbanded quickly; it is normally self-sufficient and can drive for completion without depending on the rest of the organization. Having completed one project, the team members can be moved and assimilated into another project in a continuous cycle.

More and more employees are involved in project teams of varying shapes, sizes and time spans. Such teams are generally established for a specific purpose and duration and often they are short term. Project teams can be collocated and are increasingly virtual, with members dispersed geographically.

Project teams can be established in the context of the overall corporate strategy to enhance products or services to customers, or to improve processes or change business practices in a planned and coordinated way. Equally, they can be set up to solve emerging problems or rushed into being to respond immediately to a crisis.

Membership is often determined by the objective or purpose, but generally teams are the smallest optimum size necessary for effective delivery. Team members may commit all of their contracted working time to a single project or they may be involved in multiple simultaneous projects where their expertise is required; these projects may be at different phases of their respective life cycles. An employee may be a member of a variety of teams, each with different members, project leaders and operating practices. These teams may be functional or cross-functional, with expertise drawn from across the organization or, at times, in concert with external experts from service providers or customers. Functional project teams may comprise everyone in a unit or section. In departments where there are many short-duration projects, membership may be drawn from whomever is available.

For some projects, membership is determined through selection based on specific expertise or skills, and often the project leader has autonomy to select a team of his or her choice. This may require the inclusion of giggers, bringing in specialist skills for the duration of the project. When teams are selected, leaders may have the potential to choose members they feel will work well together from a personality perspective, but too often this aspect is overlooked or even ignored.

Leadership of project teams can reflect the corporate hierarchy, meaning the most senior person is the *de facto* project leader, or the leader can be the person with the most relevant expertise. Many organizations have established a cadre of project managers who often do not have any direct reports in the traditional managerial sense but instead have leadership responsibility for all team members for the duration of a given project.

For many, a project team is not a project team unless they are deploying some sort of project management fad. For the record, **Table 9** lists some of the more well-known project management techniques out there. There is no one that is better than another; there is no obligation to use any of them. Again, it is horses for courses.

What works for one project team will not work for another. The choice of approach is determined by the nature and complexity of the project.

Table 9.
Project methodologies
(Source: The Digital Project Manager[36])

Methodology	Description
Agile	Collaborating to iteratively deliver whatever works
Scrum	Enabling a small, cross-functional, self-managing team to deliver quickly
Kanban	Improving speed and quality of delivery by increasing visibility of work in progress and limiting multi-tasking
Scrumban	Limiting work in progress, like Kanban, with a daily stand-up-like scrum
Lean	Streamlining and eliminating waste to deliver more with less
XP	Extreme programming methodology – doing development robustly to ensure quality
Waterfall	Planning projects fully and then executing through phases
PRINCE2	Controlled project management, leaving nothing to chance
PMBOK	Applying universal standards to waterfall project management

The strengths

Project management methodology aside, project teams have a clear focus, deadlines and milestones. Project goals are well defined and the commonly shorter time horizons provide an impetus to deliver. They have what other team types often lack: a clear, common objective and purpose. Indeed, the project team tends to adopt the 12 TDP criteria (see Chapter 4) of an effective team as standard – goal clarity, role clarity, leadership behaviour, participation, commitment, communication, planning, evaluation, recognition, conflict, composition and organization. This is not to suggest that they do all 12 effectively, but the project team, at its inception, tends to be more aware of these issues. The project team still needs to address each and every one of these criteria for team effectiveness on an ongoing basis.

In project teams where membership has been selected, as opposed to appointed or cobbled together based on who is available (this happens more than you would think), members will often have complementary skills. In some instances, it can be necessary to have completely diverse knowledge and experience relevant to the project and the number of members deemed appropriate to deliver.

Regardless of composition, project teams often allocate responsibilities based on capability, competency and availability. Members are aware of who owns what and the critical interdependencies between them. Knowledge of the roles allows team members to hold each other mutually accountable, to offer support where necessary and to recognize accomplishments when individuals have delivered.

The nature of projects drives the necessity to plan activities effectively from the outset. Participation by members in the initial planning helps bolster involvement and participation, enhance clarity and awareness, and facilitate the sense of control that good, well-thought-out plans provide.

The nature of project planning and control often creates a rigour of review and evaluation – Where are we? Where should we be? Regular status meetings and updates help to ensure the project stays on track and sustain the bonds between team members, the sense of *esprit de corps* and the opportunity for honest, two-way communication.

When project teams are cross-functional, members may acquire new insights from across the organization, may develop new skills and knowledge and build their networks. When members are from outside the organization, a range of different perspectives can be acquired that can add value to the individual, the team and the organization.

The challenges

Critical to the success of all project teams is mission clarity – why does this team exist? A major challenge for any project team, whether functional or cross-functional, is the focusing of team members' expectations during the forming stage. Best practice would recommend that teams are not only familiar with the mission and purpose in terms of the team's deliverables but also understand the context for the project within the organization's bigger picture. The tendency for action and to ignore the need to establish total clarity on the team goals can very quickly turn the advantages of project teams described above into a demotivating, frustrating and stressful experience.

When cross-functional teams are assembled for projects based on specific individual expertise, they need to form efficiently and effectively within a short space of time. Lack of knowledge of other team members can lead to confusion at the outset. A lack of familiarity with individual styles, the need to become acquainted with different skill sets and perhaps terminology, and the fact that the project team may have different sub-projects as part of a greater mission, all leads to confusion and impede the team's delivery. Jockeying for position and politics can also inhibit progress in the early stages, slowing down the team in reaching an effective performance level. Time must be dedicated to these aspects of forming the team and not solely the project plan.

Project leaders who are *in situ* due to their hierarchical seniority may not be the most appropriate people to manage the flexibility required for a project team. As the project progresses, leadership should be devolved. The leader should move from being the director to being the coach and facilitator. They should not undermine the maturation of the team by refusing to share leadership but instead encourage full engagement and participation of team members. Maintaining their status and reputation as the 'boss' may create a disconnect within the team, demotivating members and jeopardizing productivity.

Equally, project leaders who owe their position to technical expertise alone can fail to prioritize day-to-day people management practices, including performance management, feedback and coaching. This will be more challenging in a cross-functional team, as members who do not share the same technical background may find the leadership style inappropriate or overly utilitarian. Team members from a similar technical discipline may fully appreciate the leader's knowledge, expertise and even management style, but lose out on a balanced approach to people management.

For example, virtual project teams present significant engagement challenges for the leader, as aspects such as testing or quality assurance are often handled by different sites or countries.

In many respects, project teams have an advantage over other team types due to the in-built project review practices they commonly use. However, if the review sessions are solely focused on the plan, impending milestones and progress, they may overlook the imperative for the team to reflect on the teamwork dimension. The net result is that unhelpful behaviours, to the team and the project, can go undetected or ignored. This can have a compound effect on efficiency and delivery, including the deterioration of commitment, communication and interpersonal relations.

The imperatives

Project teams are the norm for more and more employees. For organizations to maximize the potential strengths of project teams, recognition of the inherent strengths must be accompanied by acknowledgement of the challenges.

Leaders must explain the reasons for the team's formation and its mission to members, including establishing the context and fit with the bigger picture and customer requirements. These should be reiterated at regular intervals and members' alignment confirmed. Leaders need to establish individual member expectations and set some ground rules. This includes the development of a list of agreed operating principles, and the establishment of a meeting process and evaluation formats. Leaders need to assess team training needs (knowledge of subject area, team process, tools and techniques, etc.) early in the life cycle. The leader should, as appropriate, encourage the team to determine broad approaches to the project goal and the *modus operandi* of the team.

Goal clarity is key and the team should refine the overall strategies into key goals and collectively develop detailed objectives. It is critical for leaders to ensure full understanding and support for the final goals (the project deliverables and who is the end beneficiary) from all team members. This is an essential component for all teams to be effective and is an even greater imperative when project teams comprise cross-functional representatives, giggers or members from client/customer organizations.

Leaders should recognize the need to adopt a more style-flexible approach. They must at least be conscious of the natural tendency to manage the team based on their functional seniority or technical expertise. The leader needs to acknowledge that team leadership is a multi-faceted responsibility, including project delivery and managing human capital. It is worth noting that current project management methodologies, as listed in **Table 9**, define the role of the so-called 'scrum master' in scrum (or team coach or project lead in other project methodologies) as responsible for facilitating the team, obtaining resources for it and protecting it from problems. The leader needs to provide the umbrella for the team, protecting it from damaging and interfering organizational influences, ensuring that all lines of required communication for team members with the rest of the organization are effective, timely and accessible. These tasks of leadership encompass the soft skills of project management and not the technical skills such as planning and scheduling activities, which are better left to the team as a whole.

Good planning and evaluation practices are essential. Time invested at the initial planning phase will be undermined by failure to regularly and frequently review. This will keep projects on track, identify any risks and help to maintain a sense of team purpose. Leaders should minimize the time spent in review meetings to simple status reporting. Instead they should look for opportunities to energize the team through joint problem solving and innovation linked to the project.

Leaders should encourage constructive disagreement, ensuring the team do not become complacent in their approach; the need for psychological safety is as important for this team type as any other. Ultimately, the leader needs to demonstrate that conflict within the team is an inevitability, is natural and can be a source of innovation, and that together the team need to manage it correctly to gain its benefits.

As part of the ongoing development of the team, all should find time to recognize their performance contributions, including behaviours, and to provide regular feedback to all team members. This will only happen when it is encouraged by the leader and they lead by example.

While project leaders may have one major focus on their project, they must also recognize that some team members may be involved in a number of projects, with various demands placed on them from other sources. Some participants in the team may also hold a functional role, which can place considerable tension and pressure on the individual, as satisfying two bosses is never easy. This is an issue to be resolved at the start of a project and the project leader should support team members in agreeing their project time versus their functional commitments in consultation with functional leaders.

Because team members can be involved in a number of simultaneous projects and act as technical experts, bringing a specific skill set or knowledge to the team, traditional individual performance management practices can be challenged. Team members in an intact team will generally participate in the performance management process with the full-time team leader (functional leader) to whom they report. Project team leaders may not have direct reports on their teams. They may have people assigned for the duration of the project or part of it. This may result in the leader simply contributing feedback to the direct line manager for use in the performance management process, rather than being an integral part of the goal-setting/review process. Leaders, therefore, need to plan time to contribute to performance reviews, jointly participate in goal setting, understand an individual's development goals and create opportunities for development within the context of the project.

In a final consideration, project teams would seem to have the critical factors in place to be successful. They have what other team types can lack – a clearly visible common mission and purpose. However, this alone is only a part of the recipe for success. Project teams, like all the team types, need to constantly and consistently take time out to reflect not only on 'what' they are doing but equally on 'how' they are doing it (the relationship dimensions) to ensure they give themselves the best chance of success.

Dynamic and effective when led and managed appropriately, the project team is an essential team type in the rapidly changing and evolving world of work. A hybrid of the traditional team, the project team can take on many facets. Like many of the varieties of coffee bean, it is a 'cultivar' – it is produced by techniques not normally found in natural populations. It is the Bourbon or Typica coffee bean of the team world.

Chapter 7.

The virtual team

Virtual
*Describes something that exists in essence but not in actuality;
very close to being something without actually being it;
not physically existing as such but made by technology
to appear to do so.*

The term 'virtual' applied to a team is an interesting concept based on the definition of the word above. The inference is that these teams do not really exist! Yet we know that they do, and organizations are becoming more and more dependent upon them. Maybe there is something we can take from this definition that will help with creating awareness that virtual teams are not the same as any other team. They are different in how they operate and in the way they must be led to be effective. The type of person selected for a virtual team needs additional skills and a different level of emotional intelligence to operate comfortably in the virtual world. The assumption can not be that it is just another form of the traditional or project team and can be managed and resourced in the same manner as collocated teams.

In a work context, the virtual team, geographically dispersed team, distributed team or remote team, usually refers to a group of individuals who work together from different geographical locations. They can even be from various physical locations within a building or campus. The defining feature of this kind of team is that it relies on communication technology, in its many varied forms, in order to collaborate.

The virtual team was originally conceived to facilitate innovation between experts who could not, would not or did not have the time to travel. Today the virtual team is a necessity of doing business driven by globalization, financial considerations, real estate costs, travel costs, commute times, talent availability and acquisition costs, employee flexibility demands and 24/7 operations.

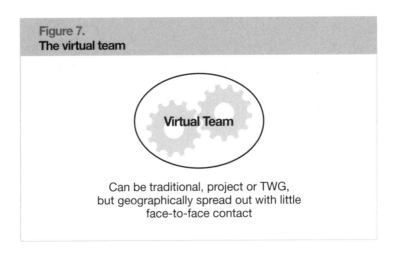

Figure 7.
The virtual team

Virtual Team

Can be traditional, project or TWG,
but geographically spread out with little
face-to-face contact

The virtual team performs the *raison d'être* of a traditional 'intact' team or project team, but rarely, if ever, a TWG (see Chapter 8). However, the essential differences are not just the team members' physical locations and the way they communicate – electronically rather than face-to-face – but also the operating or performance environment in which the team and team members exist. Those are the primary differences that drive major challenges for both the effectiveness of the team and the leadership of the team.

Although its use is increasing exponentially in terms of deployment, the virtual team does not suit all situations. Where a team relies heavily on sequential and integrated work (e.g. manufacturing) or where each person depends on what someone else is doing in the immediate term, then a virtual team cannot work. Due to the minimization of face-to-face communication and the dependency on electronic communications, virtual teams always experience a time lag when communicating and making decisions.

Many organizations have embraced the virtual team concept without considering its many challenges and have failed to develop policies and protocols to support this ever-increasing phenomenon. They are created very often in the belief that they can operate in the same manner as the collocated traditional team or project team. The many financial savings that can be accrued are lost in this failure to recognize and deal with the challenges of the virtual team.

Despite widespread growth in the use of virtual teams, little or nothing has been done to develop leaders to lead these teams. The role of the virtual leader is even more dramatic in terms of impact than it is for the collocated traditional team or project team. Virtual teams demand a greater focus from the leader in terms of developing and maintaining clear and compelling goals, performance management, communication, replacing implicit assumptions with clear rules and protocols, developing and maintaining trust between team members, delegation and fostering shared leadership. Leaders need to be specifically developed for these roles. Managing a diverse and geographically scattered team is a radically different process to managing a collocated team, where the leader can directly interact on a day-to-day basis with team members.

Equally important are the people who make up the team. Research shows that virtual teams need to recruit people with different or additional attributes that are critical to the long-term success of the team.[37] These include the capacity to be self-motivating, the ability to work independently, being comfortable working effectively without control and structure, a strong results orientation, confident and effective oral and written communication skills, and high emotional intelligence with resilience. Not everyone can work or is comfortable working in a virtual environment.

The virtual team is here to stay. It can be a great means to maximizing returns on talent. With the availability of technology, it is possible to work virtually and effectively from anywhere. Technology, however, is only an enabler; it is not an end. It only works in support of the concept when all the other issues are also correctly in place.

The strengths

Adopting a strategy that encompasses virtual teams and developing the organization and technology platforms to enable this allows talent to be sourced globally at the most competitive cost and from a wider pool. Equally, time and cost are significant gains, with less disruption to the working day, week and month, as the individual is not required to leave their workplace or travel extensively. Zero commute time for the home worker invariably sees them more productive in terms of hours worked and less stressed in terms of travel impositions.

The virtual team can deliver increased productivity and a better contribution to the bottom line. Team members tend to be more focused on the task at hand and the virtual world is a flatter world in terms of organizational structure. The reduction in bureaucracy, which tends to slow down decision making, contributes to a higher return per employee. The potential for 24/7 operations in a global team impacts product development lead times and ensures service delivery has a faster response time, serving both global and local market demands.

Decision making tends to be better where collaborative conflict management styles are developed, which is a prerequisite for a virtual team. The diversity of the group brings different perspectives and opinions, ensuring a greater range of options and leading to substantial increases in innovation. The reliance on technology also mitigates some of the challenges of diversity, e.g. email communication does not transfer accents and carries fewer noticeable language differences than verbal communication. Cultural barriers are not removed; rather, they are shielded from view where they are irrelevant.

Infrastructural cost reduction can be substantial in a well-developed virtual team strategy. Home working, in particular, drives savings in a range of areas. From a reduction in physical space required and the associated reduced facilities costs to a reduction in administrative costs and employee support services, all in all these can add up to a considerable amount.

Many job roles in the information-driven business simply do not require a person to be onsite. Technology has enabled the delivery of my entire business in a virtual environment and we benefit from the associated cost savings. Attrition rates can be lowered, with employees enjoying a better work-life balance, delivering a substantial saving on recruitment, training and the loss of developed intellectual capital that walks out that door every time someone leaves.

The challenges

Cultural diversity can have negative impacts when not managed or appreciated, from simply failing to recognize national holidays to more complex issues surrounding language barriers and inter-pretation. Styles of communication can also have an impact, with some cultures practising very direct communication and others finding this uncomfortable. The generation gap can be highlighted in this kind of team, as older members may struggle with the virtual environment whereas younger members may feel immedi-ately comfortable with the technology. Time zones can become a critical and contentious flash point if not managed fairly in terms of meetings, deadlines and project deliverables.

Satisfaction tends to be lower in the virtual team, in part due to lower levels of trust between team members. Without face-to-face communication, trust is more difficult to establish and maintain. Lojeski and Reilly (2008)[38] found that virtual teams, where the organization did not develop a coherent strategy to meet the challenges of the virtual world, could suffer a decline in performance by as much as 50%, innovation by 93%, satisfac-tion by 80% and trust by 83%. The gains made can be quickly lost and the supposed financial benefits become a cost rather than a saving.

Transactive memory rarely exists in the virtual team and is not transmitted to new members, so contextual knowledge is not kept or readily available. A transactive memory system consists of the knowledge stored in each individual's memory combined with an understanding of different team members' areas of expertise. Just as an individual is aware of what information is available for retrieval within themselves, the transactive memory system provides team members with information regarding the knowledge they have access to within the team.[34] Team members learn who the knowledge experts are and how to access expertise through their communication processes, both formal and informal. In this way, a transactive memory system can provide the team with more and better knowledge than any individual could access on their own. Collocated traditional and project teams develop this intuitively due to their day-to-day, face-to-face communication. The virtual team needs to create this artificially and consciously work at ensuring its availability and transmission.

Virtual team members must operate more independently than the traditional team. This calls for increased delegation and shared leadership. This infers a requirement for higher levels of trust and processes that support both the leader and the team member. The required independence of the team in terms of their operations can lead to isolation and issues of belonging, impacting morale and motivation. Leaders need to pay attention to this aspect. When part of the team is collocated and others are remote, it can have a significant impact, with remote members quickly feeling left out.

Membership creep is a phenomenon of the virtual team. Individuals can be invited to contribute on a specific issue and suddenly are on every call. The team grows without anyone being sure how it happened and confusion reigns. I refer you to Chapter 3 and the importance of team size. Managing external and specialized contributors is essential.

The imperatives

Virtual teams can be very effective, but it must never be assumed that they are simply another traditional or project team. To maximize the potential from this type of team, the organization needs to develop a clear and unambiguous strategy that recognizes the uniqueness of the virtual team and the fact that, as a team type, it has very particular demands if it is to be successful. Enabling technology platforms alone is not the answer.

Recognizing the issues of size, that bigger is *not* better, and managing membership creep are of paramount importance. Assertively managing membership creep, and developing rules and protocols for who should be at a virtual team meeting and why, is an essential task and not one normally associated with the traditional team or project team. The team composition must be continually reassessed for its suitability. When assembling a virtual team, pay attention to the individual attributes required, as previously outlined.

Clear goals and roles for the virtual team are essential. There can no room for ambiguity. This is a leader responsibility and it must not only be done at the outset, but continually reinforced and re-clarified. Goals must be compelling to maintain a sense of purpose and direction for team members. Traditional and project teams have the opportunity day-to-day to correct goal drift or wandering priorities. In contrast, the virtual world can have days, even weeks, without immediate contact and drift is a real issue. While goal clarity is an important issue for any team, it is even more so for this team type.

Leaders need specialized training to lead and manage a virtual team. This team type is not the same as regular collocated teams and requires a different mindset and approach from the leader. Advanced skills in delegation, fostering shared leadership, goal setting, role clarification, communication and performance management are essential for an effective virtual team leader. The leader must also be trained in all technology to be deployed and capable of understanding any issue that may arise. None of the foregoing are a given and the organization must address them to have an effective virtual team. No one should be asked to lead a virtual team without the appropriate development and training.

With such a variety of high-end technology available to teams, the emphasis can often be on the technology at the expense of all other considerations, and on providing the most advanced and sophisticated available at that. Some geographical locations may not have the bandwidth or infrastructure to support the most advanced technology and this puts team members in those locations at a disadvantage. Many home workers are working through 'domestic' ranges of connectivity and can find it impossible to reach the required bandwidth, particularly when it comes to upload speeds. Data sharing facilities form a vital element of the virtual team, particularly in helping to address the issues of transactive memory and contextual knowledge. There are many choices, so pick the one that works best for the team involved. Some are dedicated to sending and hosting large files in a corporate context – Hightail, MediaFire, RapidShare and ShareFile, for example. Others are more general, personal-use file-storage services that have mass distribution as an adjunct feature – Box, Dropbox, Google Drive, Minus, OneDrive and SugarSync. Whichever is adopted, make sure that not only can all team members access it, in terms of both upload and download speeds, but also that they know how to use it. Equally, the generation gap must also be respected in terms of technology deployed, which has implications for training and commissioning the team in the first instance.

Communication rules are essential. When the team needs to meet virtually is one thing, and the rules of engagement are essential, but equally important is the direct communication between members via phone, email, texts and instant messaging services such as Slack and Teamwork Chat. It is equally important to establish standards in this area – timely responses, content, sensitivity to cultural differences, recognition of time differences and many more.

There are key variables and stages that must be addressed for the virtual team to enable effective functioning. These are not 'nice to dos'; they are essential. First and foremost in assembling a virtual team is the 'kick off' and socializing of team members – affording time for them to get to know each other and the roles they will play in the team. Despite the virtual nature of the team, the team should come together physically, at the very least once a year and preferably once a quarter. This has a major impact on trust and *esprit de corps* for the team. This does have cost implications in terms of travel and accommodation, but the investment pays off in creating a team bond and allowing team members to get to know each other. I would say this is an essential first step for any new virtual team. The more this can be done in the life cycle of the team, the better. Varying the location of the meeting geographically is also good practice, giving team members an opportunity to introduce and share their respective cultures.

Ensuring a robust induction process for new members to the team is an absolute, particularly when a new member joins and there is no planned physical meet. A mentor or buddy system, and making time available for new members to meet with existing team members on a virtual but individual basis, is essential.

Clarification of not only goals and roles but also tasks and processes is something that must be scheduled for at both the team and individual levels. If ever there is a need for the principles of inverted hierarchy leadership, it is in the virtual team. The leader must be aware of any and all possible impediments to the performance of both the team and individual members, and check for these at both levels on a regular basis. Allied to this is the need to establish milestones embedded in robust planning and evaluation practices to enable a sense of progression and achievement, which is a critical for the virtual team.

Developing a set of rules of engagement together and committing to these rules without exception is critical for the virtual team. It is a major contributor to establishing a safe psychological environment, sets expectations on behaviours and goes a long way towards mitigating the impact of minor or small transgressions of the psychological contract that could otherwise blow out of all proportion. It also helps to accommodate cultural differences, minimizing misunderstandings.

So much of a virtual team's success is dependent on the leader. This extends beyond performance management and operational issues to the leader's availability on an individual basis and their capacity to recognize the success and contributions of each team member. Most importantly, developing true delegation (responsibility with power), engendering trust between team members and between the team leader and team members is a must.

While the former are essential for all teams, they become more critical for the virtual team and where any one of them is overlooked there is a much greater impact. The collocated team has many informal opportunities to overcome the absences of any of the above, while such opportunities are not available to the virtual team.

In a final consideration, organizations must recognize that the virtual team is not the same as other teams and the same approach, strategies and processes will not work. Team leaders must be developed specifically to lead these teams for the organization to gain the best return. Virtual teams, by their nature, require a greater focus on rules, protocols and regulations. These should be developed by the team and not imposed. The virtual team needs to be more formal in its operation.

People are social in nature and when forced to work alone may struggle with isolation and miss many of the things taken for granted in a traditional workplace. The sharing of information around the coffee machine, the water cooler or even the smoking shed is denied to the virtual employee. This cuts them off from practically all of the informal communication processes of the organization. Our sense of belonging is not just derived from our team but from the organization overall. Our sense of security and engagement, along with our ever-present need to socialize (often taken for granted), is met by the informal environment of the organization and our place of employment. One should compensate for these factors and consciously plan to manage the many vagaries of the virtual world.

The virtual team is the Robusta coffee bean of the team world. Yes, it is a variation of the traditional team or project team (so still coffee, still a team) but, in reality, it is a completely different breed and this must be recognized. The Robusta bean tastes different and has nearly double the caffeine. The green bean of Robusta is also about half the cost of the Arabica green bean. For sure, the virtual team is the Robusta bean of the team world.

Chapter 8.

Teaming work group

> **Teaming**
> *A way of working relating to, or performed by, a team;*
> *a number of persons associated in some joint action;*
> *the activity of working together as a team.*

The word 'teaming' has entered the parlance of the world of work in recent years and can be defined as a verb (action), as above, or as a noun, as in the type of team under discussion here. Teaming is the 'verbing' of the noun 'team', which is not uncommon practice in English, and has transitioned since its adoption in the workplace to become part of a noun – 'teaming work group' – in its own right. So why the grammar lesson? The concept is somewhat confusing. There are teaming cultures (noun) and teaming work groups (noun), and teaming is seen as a way of working (verb), as a dynamic activity and not a static or bounded entity. The preceding chapters considered teams from a static, bounded perspective. In this chapter, the teaming work group (TWG) is also being considered from this perspective, so I am using the term as part of a noun, but at times I will use it as a verb.

In her book *Teaming: How Organizations Learn, Innovate and Compete in the Knowledge Economy*[39] Amy Edmondson has called on managers to stop thinking of teams as static groups of individuals who have ample time to practise interacting successfully and effectively. Rather, she recommends embracing teaming as a verb, developing it as an essential skill for all and seeing it as the mindset and practice of teamwork, and not the design and structure of effective teams. I absolutely agree with this. Teaming skills should be imbued in an organization as part of a CTS, but there is still a need to consider teams in terms of the static and bounded rationale and ensure that they do have the time to be reflective on how they do things.

The TWG is a growing phenomenon in organizations today. It is essentially a traditional 'intact' team, a functional team (occasionally a project team and very rarely a virtual team), with the all-important difference being its composition. Based around shifts, the team is never comprised of the same people two shifts running. This team type is to be found in many organizations today, for example hospitals, airlines, call centres, retail (shop floor), hotel and tourism, and fast food.

The concept has developed in response to shift patterns, the need for 24/7 operations, zero-hour contracts and growing flexibility demands from employees in terms of hours worked. In such industries as the airline industry, keeping the same flight crew (team) together is not financially practical and algorithms are used to maximize utilization of both employees and aircraft, where each is perceived as an individual unit. The net result is that employees seldom work with the same colleagues. This can mean that where two colleagues are assigned to work on the same trip or flight for a major airline, it could be as many as five years before it would happen again.

Many organizations today will have a pool of people that they will draw from to generate a shift or to meet the demands of a 24/7 operation. In effect, the 'team' can be 100 people or more with maybe only 10 to 15 of that pool working on any given shift or in any given period. This may seem to go against earlier

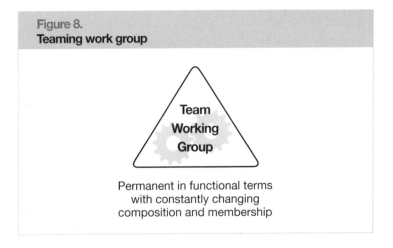

Figure 8.
Teaming work group

Team
Working
Group

Permanent in functional terms
with constantly changing
composition and membership

suggestions that team size should not be in double digits. The reality is, however, that this can happen. My earlier comments were as much to emphasize the issues associated with double digits and the need to address and manage the problems that arise when team size goes beyond the magical double-digit threshold. In most instances, where there are more than ten members, the likelihood is that there are two or more actual teams in play. This a factor to be considered, particularly in the TWG shift composition.

This type of team is becoming more and more common. It has substantial advantages but also enormous challenges. This type of grouping still needs to exhibit teaming behaviours, maybe even as a greater imperative due to the constant change in composition. Developing and maintaining robust team standards and protocols is difficult with the TWG.

It stands to reason that a team that has stable composition will learn, develop protocols, deal with mistakes collectively and, in effect, develop a history that informs further actions (transactive memory). This is not available to the TWG in the same way that it is to some other types of team. It is not possible to develop this type of group in a traditional team development paradigm. Intervention is not possible in the same manner when a problem arises. The more an organization depends on this type of team (which is growing exponentially), the more it faces an increase in errors and mistakes. So how does one support this type of organization and ensure that the TWG is as effective as any other form of team?

The strengths

The TWG is a variant of the traditional team and some of the strengths of the traditional team apply. Specialists still work together providing support for in-depth competence with many people talking the same operational language. It is similarly easier to attract specialization to this type of team. Specialists tend to appreciate working with like-minded individuals who share their 'business speak' and are more likely to share their world views.

This type of traditional grouping also benefits from efficiency in terms of resources, where equipment and people are clustered centrally as the TWG is predominantly collocated.

As with traditional teams, there is freedom to focus on the task at hand while others do the coordination, providing the opportunity for each team member to maximize what they do best. Management structures above the team member take care of the broader concerns and issues.

The chain of command is clear, communication flows are delineated on the vertical axis, job roles are clear and centred on tasks, and the individual is recruited to the team based on specific task skills. The stable and clear structure is a major contributor to a team member's sense of clarity and job purpose. Change in this TWG environment is comparably slower than in other team types, and quick responses to change are not always essential, further contributing to clarity and job purpose.

This team type does provide a financial advantage in respect of labour costs, both in terms of unitization and the nature of zero-hour contracts, which often accompany this team structure. It also enables a more effective delivery of a 24/7 operation, ensuring that a full complement of staff is always available. However, the apparent financial savings can be entirely offset by the challenges of this team type, seeing it become the costliest of team types.

Establishing a large pool of employees to draw from increases the variation of skill sets and perspectives and, if properly captured, can create a valuable base of knowledge and experience beyond that of more traditional team structures. This also delivers a flexibility to employees that would not available under traditional contracts of employment.

The challenges

The TWG presents more challenges in my experience than any other team type.

Maintaining standards of performance is more difficult in this team structure. Performance differences, allied to differences in standards, are inevitable. Drawing a relatively small but constantly changing group from a large pool means differences in approach, personality, attitude and experience. These may be in some instances subtle and in others more obvious. Nonetheless, the impact for the customer in a service context can be substantial.

Delivering an appropriate leadership style is challenging for team leaders as they never work with the same team. The mix of personalities, levels of skill and competencies continually fluctuates and puts considerable pressure on the team leader. The converse is also true – team members have to deal with different leaders on an ongoing basis who prioritize and lead differently; what is considered a must for one team leader may be anathema to another. This can be very stressful for the team member. It can be a major demotivator as it is often perceived as capricious decision making. The best way to deal with that is to keep your head below the parapet and do nothing. At least that way you do not run the risk of offending anyone!

Error rates and mistakes are predictably higher as team members do not have the opportunity to establish norms or develop transactive memory.[34] Traditional teams do this intuitively, but the TWG does not have the same facility. This alone is a major contributor to the error rate. TWGs do not have the same opportunities to learn from mistakes. Hospital ward teams (which I consider TWGs) manage this through robust shift change-over practices along with continuing education. For many organizations this doesn't happen and shifts in many instances do not overlap.

Team or collective training is difficult, as the continuous shuffling of team composition makes it tricky to recognize a specific issue that requires an intervention. What is a problem for one combination of people may never appear again, unless the exact group is by chance scheduled again. Individual training is possible but can only address common features such as rules, regulations, health and safety, and so on. The traditional team and project team can address how certain identified challenges impact their operation, errors and problems and deal with them – the TWG cannot do so.

The constant change in composition impedes the ability of team members to develop closer working relationships, building on each other's strengths and weaknesses. This also impacts the team members' sense of engagement, ownership and belonging, ultimately resulting in greater attrition and turnover, and lower levels of morale and motivation. The sense of *esprit de corps* is always less in this team structure. Performance management becomes a challenge in the context of the TWG employee, where day-to-day leaders may not be the reviewer and the reviewer may not be aware of performance accomplishments or failures; in addition, the review may not be timely. While there is a financial advantage in utilization and labour cost, there is a converse side of increased costs in terms of turnover, decreased morale and motivation, increased error rates, increased administrative requirements and the many related costs that thereby accrue to the organization.

The imperatives

TWGs are becoming more common, but many organizations have not developed the strategies to fully support this team type and mitigate the negatives associated with it. In many cases, the traditional approach to team development will not work. Even identifying the issues that should be addressed can be difficult. Leadership is more challenging in this structure and this brings its own set of challenges for how leaders are developed.

Due to the large size of the pool being drawn from to people a shift or work period, it is extremely difficult to bring the entire complement of staff together to discuss their challenges and maintain the sense of team spirit that encourages commitment. These barriers ultimately impact innovation, drive and even passion for the work to be done in the most effective manner.

To maximize the potential, the organization must develop a clear strategy for this team type. Although it is a derivative of the traditional team, the challenges are very different.

Leadership development must take account of the continuing change in composition and, in this scenario, leaders must be more capable of recognizing the need for flexibility in terms of their leadership style. This must flex to meet the needs of team members on a continuous basis, from directive to supportive, and from encouragement to delegation. Leaders must come to terms with the understanding of matching leadership style to subordinate readiness and capability. It is assuredly not an environment where one style fits all. This is not something that most leaders can do naturally. They need help to develop introspection, understand their preferred style and learn to flex. The large pool to be drawn from to form a shift inevitably means that team members will vary widely in terms of experience, capacity and even basic skills. This becomes the leader's problem once the shift is in place and they must manage and lead the shift for the next eight hours. This is a primary example of where behavioural-type instruments can be deployed to help a team leader understand their natural and supporting styles and develop strategies for flexibility in leadership style.

The organization must build an understanding of the challenges that emerge for this type of team. Take the hospital ward and a continuous shift cycle as an example. Are the challenges the same on the night shift as they are on the day or evening shift? What kind of issues are emerging that the overall group need to be aware of? One approach is to use a team development instrument to capture team members' experiences as they come off a shift. Once a quarter, if this is done across the continuous shift cycle, a picture can be built up to understand the different issues and patterns that emerge in relation to the different shifts. If this is then correlated with other data – for example, with ongoing patient feedback – a comprehensive picture can be established of typical challenges faced by the group overall.

This will not necessarily feed into a training intervention but rather into briefing sessions for the team members as they rotate through their shifts. It can provide objective data and information for the team members from themselves and allow them to develop strategies to address the issues over time.

Consideration should be given to bringing the extended group together on a regular basis. This is challenging and its feasibility will often be determined by operational demands and constraints. Failing that, a regular quarterly session should be made available for team members to attend to discuss the challenges of working in this environment. This does not need to be the entire pool, but one would hope that over a 12-month period the vast majority will have been included and have been afforded the opportunity to air their views.

As with other team types, goals, roles and the other prerequisites of effective teams need to be constantly reinforced. This is where an organizational approach to teaming as a way of working will help, where teaming skills are expected of everyone and integrated into all training initiatives. This should include understanding conflict and how to deal with it, maintaining flexibility and the ability to identify moments of collaboration as they appear, recognizing interdependence and when it is needed, and learning how to coordinate between individuals and teams.

In a final consideration, one must bear in mind that a TWG is for all intents and purposes a traditional team, but not all the strengths apply and there are certainly more challenges. I suspect that these challenges greatly increase the actual financial cost of this team type. Despite the previous assertion that there are financial savings to be made with this team type, there is a propensity for error, there are complications in training, and there is much higher attrition due to issues of morale, motivation, which leads to knowledge loss and inconsistency of output to end users. I believe these factors drive the costs of this team type to levels we have not even begun to investigate. The complicating impact of the ever-changing composition must never be underestimated.

All teams have common attributes and all teams can be considered unique. Organizations deploying this team type must develop a support strategy that reflects the needs of their TWGs to deliver effectiveness and minimize financial impact.

> **The TWG is unique, and its characteristics and challenges are very different from those of the other team types. It takes a lot more effort, care and investment in time to deliver an effective TWG. The TWG is the Kopi Luwak coffee bean of the team world. This bean is unique and the most expensive coffee type, primarily because of the time it takes to be produced. The bean is collected only after it has passed through the digestive tract of the palm civet or 'toddy cat'. The TWG can be effective but requires considerably more time and financial investment from the organization overall than other team types. Once established, other team types can be self-developing; the TWG requires continuous investment and support.**

Part 3.

Making a great cup of coffee

Based on the TDP model (see the model in Chapter 4), there are 12 criteria that drive team effectiveness. Any team that consistently addresses the related issues will improve their overall performance and effectiveness. TDP is a factor model of team life with six factors, each comprised of two criteria. This part of the book takes each of the factors and their two criteria and explores their nature, explaining the importance and impact of each for the team. The implications for morale and motivation are also examined and the link to each criterion established.

TDP is an integrated model of team life. Each of the constituent elements interacts with all of the others. Address one area of the model and you will impact most other areas. If you move one cog, all the other cogs will rotate. Therefore, by necessity, there is overlap and some duplication in the chapters that follow. Apologies in advance.

Part 3 is designed to help the team address the issues that can impede effective performance and offers a series of questions a team should ask and answer for themselves, to formulate action plans to improve their effectiveness. If this is done on an ongoing basis, there will be continuous and incremental improvement in performance. If it is done in an inclusive manner, where all participate, it will greatly support the issues of psychological safety and create an environment of continuous learning, leading to innovation and engagement.

This is not an approach that tells the team what to do and it does not offer magic formulas or silver bullets. It is a methodology that provides a structure for and focus on the key aspects of team effectiveness and recognizes that teams, for the most part, hold the answers themselves to driving effectiveness. They just need time to step back and consider 'how' they work, determine what gaps exist for them and how they believe these gaps can be closed.

Absolutely, there will be times when a team needs outside support, but 90% of what they need to drive their effectiveness they can deliver for themselves. The methodology is not a 'big bang' approach – you will not address all issues in one session. It is about developing a discipline that enables the team, with a clear structure, to continually assess their performance, plan actions and assess again. It is a true action learning cycle.

This is the 'making the coffee' part of the book. If you want good coffee that works for the whole team, you have to get team member's input on what they like. You have to try out different types, different blends and different ways of making it produce the right beverage for the team. It takes time, it takes effort, but it is worth the investment for that perfect brew.

Chapter 9.

Goal and role clarity

Goal clarity

> **Goal**
> *An observable and measurable end result,*
> *having one or more objectives to be achieved*
> *within a more or less fixed time frame.*

> **"If you don't know where you are going**
> **you will end up someplace else."**
> Yogi Berra

Goal clarity appears simple and is simple, yet many teams get it wrong. It is the baseline for team performance. Setting goals for teams is no different from setting them for an individual. The principles of the performance management cascade apply equally to a team setting. Teams by their nature are task oriented or, more accurately stated, activity oriented. They want to 'do' things.

When presented with a simple task in the training room (e.g. to build a high, stable structure with straws and paper clips that will survive a test of robustness), a team will often jump straight in without thinking first about what needs to be achieved. They will start putting straws and paper clips together as they talk about what needs to happen. Some in the team will be working on the principle of stability, some on the principle of height and some on the test of robustness. They are not aligned, have not thought through the goal, have no plan, have not considered the challenges in depth and invariably realize that their structure will not meet the criteria when the time limit has expired.

It could be suggested what is described above is more a function of planning and evaluation. To an extent this is true, but without clear goals there is nothing to plan and evaluate. In fact, goal clarity is the baseline for all team performance. Without a clear path of where we are going, why we are going there, how we will get there, when we will get there and what getting there looks like, all other aspects of team performance are inaccessible.

Without goal clarity, team roles cannot be determined, team structure (what skills are required) cannot be established, planning and evaluation techniques cannot be appropriately selected, an appropriate leadership style cannot be delivered, communication and decision-making methods cannot be clarified, and individual performance and contribution cannot be assessed. They all require a goal as the starting point.

Goal clarity is not a 'one off'. It is important to constantly clarify the goals of any team. It is not unusual to have a team claim goal clarity and then find that, when members are challenged individually on the goals of the team, they express a differing and even contradictory understandings of the goals. This can lead to wasted effort, duplication of tasks, incorrect prioritization, some tasks not being performed at all, and frustration and confusion. It is certainly not an environment where a team can achieve its most effective state.

Goal clarity not only impacts all aspects of effectiveness, but also provides the road map, the vision of what success looks like; it is essential in uniting the team effort to reach the common goal. The team's goal process is, in essence, no different to an organization's goal process or indeed the performance management process. It is, however, specific to the team and must be carried out as an independent exercise. There are a series of questions that must be answered and clearly understood by all team members. The questioning process is not just a first step but must be repeated at regular intervals. It must never be assumed that the goals are clear and that every team member interprets them in the same way. Communicating goals just once is never enough.

For many, it may seem like overkill and unnecessary to constantly remind team members of goals, but it is a critical task of leadership. If these are not continuously reaffirmed, any team will be less than effective in terms of its capability. It will likely end up somewhere other than where it intended to be in the first instance.

Teams with and without goal clarity display the characteristics outlined in **Table 10** below. Review them and ask yourself, "Where is my team in respect of these characteristics?" If your team is displaying any of the characteristics on the left-hand side, the team has an issue with goal clarity.

Table 10.
Team goal characteristics

Teams without goal clarity	Teams with goal clarity
Appear disorganized and even inept	Appear organized and purposeful
Are constantly under pressure and struggle with time	Are more economical in terms of effort
Develop higher levels of stress	Experience less stress
Can experience fractious and argumentative relationships	Enjoy better relationships, internally and externally
Find overtime is the norm	Work less overtime
Tend to achieve less	Are capable of achieving more
Cannot plan or evaluate effectively	Can plan and evaluate with accuracy
Either underutilize or overburden their assets	Experience greater utilization of their assets
Find on-time delivery almost impossible and it happens by accident rather than design	Are more likely to deliver on time
Have higher turnover and absenteeism	Suffer less turnover of membership
Experience poor communication and participation	Can deliver better engagement with all team members
Have ambiguous accountability and hence performance management becomes impossible	Can manage individual performance with accuracy
Find pride and loyalty to the team is undermined	Engender loyalty
Are less effective and struggle to deliver success	Are more effective and ultimately more successful

Questions and actions to be addressed by the team and leader

Teams need to address goals at two levels – at the team level and
then, and only then, at the individual level, ensuring that individual goals align with team goals. There is only one way to do
this properly and it involves the team in a discussion based on the
following questions. This is not an exhaustive list but if, as a team,
you can answer all these questions you will greatly enhance the
level of team goal clarity.

- Why do we exist? What is our purpose? – The vision that empha-
  sizes the overall purpose and ethos of the team.
- What do we need to achieve in the immediate term? – The mis-
  sion for the immediate future.
- When do we need to achieve this? – The deadline.
- Why do we need to achieve this? – Benefits, impact, importance
  and consequences of failure.
- What are the objectives (sub-goals) that need to be achieved?
  – The key milestones that inform the team of overall progress.
- Who or what is the end beneficiary of the goal(s)? – Ourselves,
  another department, the organization overall, a customer, a
  combination of these?
- What does success look like? How will we know we are there? –
  The standards to be established and what provides impetus and
  drive to complete tasks.
- Have the goals changed recently or are they relatively static? –
  New projects, new team remit or is it business as usual?
- How does the team deal with changes to the goals? – Formal
  process, one-to-one, at a team level or through project planning adjustments?
- Are the goals all recorded and accessible/visible to all? – Central registry, hard or soft copy, at the individual level and
  shared by members between themselves, or openly discussed
  at team meetings?
- Are team goals and individual goals aligned? – One-to-one in a
  discussion with the leader or a team-level discussion?

- How often does the team/team leader review goal progress? – Weekly, monthly, quarterly? Is the review interval appropriate?
- How often does performance feedback occur? What form does it take? – Informal chats on a weekly basis, quick 'check-ins' via technology or formal performance meetings on a monthly or quarterly basis?
- How do team members reconcile individual work goals and team goals when priorities have to be made? – With or without the support of the team leader?

Suggested approaches

In the first instance, goal clarity is very much the responsibility of the team leader. Teams want to know what is expected of them and they want it communicated clearly and unambiguously. The leader must lead the discussion with the team on purpose, goals and deliverables and how, in turn, they link to delivering the business' goals. This will help to identify and develop the team's vision and mission statement. The most effective manner in which to do this is to focus on the team's customers (internal and external) and how the team's performance impacts the service given to and retention of customers.

Having established team goals, cascade these to each individual by holding an objective-setting meeting with each employee to re-articulate them and to agree individual objectives for a period (e.g. quarterly). Monitor and review progress and follow through with each member each period. Regularly review how the team is working and what it is delivering against the perceived/required demands of the team. Assume people will forget the goals and objectives, so keep reminding them.

Make sure that the team's goals are integrated into work programmes and individual objectives; revisit the goals of the team when the organization's goals or structure change. This will ensure that the team's goals remain fully relevant and that the team can integrate their goals with internal changes. Monitor progress against team goals on a weekly or monthly basis by putting measures in place to track progress against the goals. Always ensure

that recognition is provided when individual team members or
the team make an achievement related to delivery of the goals.
Equally, never fail to address and understand why a particular
objective has not been delivered and adjust the plan accordingly.

Goal clarity looks simple and is simple. All it takes is reasoned
thinking, engagement with the team member on a one-to-one
basis and with the team overall in a group session, continuous
reaffirmation through communication, and not a whole lot of
time. For the return that it will deliver, it is well worth the effort.

A question of morale or motivation?

Goal clarity is without doubt a question of morale. Remember,
morale is all about wanting to belong to a group, or team in
this instance – the sense of *esprit de corps*. If a person does not
know why the group exists and how they fit into it, how can they
decide they want to belong? Goals and goal clarity are linked to
two key features of morale, common purpose and confidence in
the future, without which one cannot experience morale. If, as a
team leader, you were to simply focus on issues of morale, ignoring all else in terms of team models, best practice guidelines and
so on, you would still have to address the issues of goal clarity as
described previously, if you wanted to create the conditions for
morale to be experienced.

Common purpose is essential for a sense of group or team purpose. This can only happen by developing a clear sense of purpose
for a team – a vision. This is in addition to team mission and members' personal goals and is about the *raison d'être* of the team or unit.
You will be surprised how many teams lack this critical element. For
a common purpose to exist in terms of morale, it must be unambiguous and relatable, and all team members must be able to articulate
it in the same manner. Others outside the team should be able to
clearly understand what the team is about and what it does. Without a clear sense of common purpose, there is no obvious reason for
a team to exist and no binding reason for the team to stay together
– no morale, no *esprit de corps*, no reason for wanting to belong.

Confidence in the future also relates to the mission of the team and the overall environment in which the team exists.

Is the mission relatable? Is it achievable? Is it challenging and interesting for the team members? Will it sustain the team over time (the operational period)? Does it have real meaning for the organization overall? Is what the team is doing important to the organization and is this recognized by the organization? Nothing undermines morale more than a lack of confidence in the future.

Being achievable and relatable are important attributes for any team mission. If the team members do not believe it can be achieved, their confidence will immediately be undermined. Remember the old maxim – whether you believe you can or you can't, you're right!

If the team believes it is unimportant to the organization over-all, if the team is threatened with disbandment, if there is constant reorganization happening, and if the organizational environment is unstable and threatens individual security in terms of job tenure, then morale will be undermined. People will not want to belong, and their focus will be on securing continuity, tenure and job security, including finding it someplace else.

Key focus for the team leader: Take time to involve the team members in a group session to determine the mission. It does not need to be complicated; in fact, the clearer and simpler the statement, the better in terms of clarity. The mission is a statement of the group's core objectives in any given operational period. The mission statement clearly states the focus by determining what is important and what is not; clearly states who or what will be served and how; and, most importantly, communicates a sense of intended direction for the group. Any individual should be able to read the mission and understand what they need to do in their job to support and deliver the mission.

Once a mission is established, the team leader needs to focus on the individual team members' goals in terms of their role in delivery. The goals of all team members should be related to each other and it is the collective achievement of the team members' goals that delivers the team mission.

Having a vision, mission and goals is the only way to develop a common purpose and establish confidence for the future. Without the effort and focus on these important elements, one cannot expect to create a sense of common purpose and confidence. All are essential for morale to be experienced.

Regularly reinforce the team vision and mission, and ensure that all team members and new joiners fully understand it. Broadcast the team's mission to other teams and engage with other team leaders where there is interaction and interdependency, ensuring that those around the team understand the team's challenge. In reporting team output, recognize team members' input and contributions by team member name and ensure their recognition by the organization. If there is change happening around the team, focus on understanding that change and communicate it to the team. Even when the future is unclear, keep a dialogue going with the team in terms of what you know and strive to remove the uncertainty as much as possible. In a vacuum, when there is a lack of communication, team members will fill the void with the rumour machine. This is seldom accurate and can severely undermine confidence.

Goal clarity is all about determining which coffee you are going to drink and why. Will you have percolated coffee? Will you have instant? Will you grind your own fresh beans? Having made that choice, you then have to determine which type and which brand. All those decisions then have implications for making the coffee and how easy or complicated the process will be. Goal setting is no different. Both need discussion, consideration of the alternatives, understanding of the implications, and consensus decision. Ultimately, the overall appropriateness must be reviewed on an ongoing basis.

Role clarity

Role

The way in which someone is involved in an activity, situation or status in a group or organization, and how much influence they have on it.

"Clarity affords focus."
Thomas Leonard

Role ambiguity is one of the greatest sources of stress. Though easily fixed, it is an ongoing issue for many teams. Teams with role clarity are substantially more successful than teams without.

Role clarity assumes goal clarity. Yet, even when teams have established goal clarity, many struggle with role clarity. Teams have even been observed arguing about who is on a team and who is not! This is a more common phenomenon then one would expect.

An individual's team role clarity is a prerequisite for effective team performance. A team member's functional role or their job description may be subtly or very different to their team role. There will also be times when the two are the same. It is important to establish and clearly communicate if there are differences. When team members know what is expected of them, which aspects of their role are most important, how the delivery of that role contributes to team goals and how their performance will be evaluated, the team as a whole will perform to a higher level of effectiveness. However, this is not just a case of individual role clarity; each team member must also be clear on the roles of all other team members. This requires regular discussion between the team and team leader, with the leader ensuring that individually and collectively all team members understand their own and each other's roles.

It is not uncommon to hear a team leader say, "What do you mean 'low role clarity'? They all have their job descriptions!" Job descriptions are a requirement but are insufficient in themselves. For most employees, a job description is the document against which they were recruited. It is a defined 'job' within the organization. However, it does not necessarily define their role in a team. Clarity and definition of a team role is an iterative process that requires ongoing discussion between the leader and team members, as well as among team members.

In *Coaching for Improved Work Performance* (2002), Ferdinand Fournies reports, from a survey of 25,000 managers and supervisors, that the number one reason for people not doing what they are supposed to do is that "they don't know what they are supposed to do".[40] This is clearly linked to role clarity.

If goal clarity is the bedrock of all team activity, then role clarity is absolutely the platform that defines expectations, enables performance management and holds team members accountable. Role clarity is the means by which priorities can be mapped and training needs are understood. It ensures that all team members contribute fully in terms of their capabilities.

The effective team leader, seeking to lead an effective team, will commit time and effort to this crucial element of teamwork. They will not simply define the roles on paper and hand them out. They will explain each role and ensure that its purpose and deliverables are clearly understood in a broad context. A leader must ensure that the expectations of each role are understood by both the 'role owner' and other team members. They must also identify, clarify and manage organizational challenges that impact each role. Just telling people to act as a team is not enough, if the organizational constraints prevent them from acting as a team. Role clarity is an ongoing maintenance task and it is the responsibility of the leader and not the team members.

Without role clarity, confusion reigns within the team and repetition of tasks and resource wastage are common features. It is inevitable that tasks will fall between the cracks. High performance is impossible as individuals must now operate in a vacuum.

Without role clarity, performance and accountability cannot be managed and certainly not in an objective and fair manner. Some individuals will end up 'carrying' others, which will lead to perceptions of unfairness. This, in turn, can lead to a breakdown in trust and, ultimately, in the sense of team spirit.

Teams without role clarity cannot be effective or successful. If they are, then it is purely by chance. Without role clarity, teams and team members do not know what to prioritize or where to focus their efforts, nor do they understand if their performance is acceptable. In short, they don't know what they are doing. Check **Table 11** on the next page and see if your team needs to address any issues of role clarity.

Questions and actions to be addressed by the team and leader

Individual role clarity, leading to overall team role clarity, is not an obvious or straightforward task. There is no one or best or pre-scribed means to establish role clarity. It involves discussion with the team members on an individual basis and as a collective and it is mostly concerned with actions. Goal clarity requires a series of questions to be answered by the team before any actions on role clarity can be initiated (see previous section – Goal clarity).

The team leader needs to be cognizant of team members' status in terms of whether the roles have changed or whether they are relatively static. It is equally important to recognize that, as goals change, previous understanding of roles may no longer be valid. It is critically important that individual team members not only understand their own role but also that of other team members. Where concerns are expressed in terms of role clarity, it is important to understand what is not clear – the individual's understanding of their own role or their under-standing of other roles. It is essential to support team members to reconcile individual work goals and team goals when pri-orities have to be made to help avoid confusion and ambigu-ity and the resultant stress this can cause to a team member.

Table 11.
Team role characteristics

Teams without role clarity		Teams with role clarity	
Are disorganized		Are organized and purposeful	
Lack focus		Are focused	
Are fractious and distrustful of each other		Have clear and supportive relationships	
Are constantly seeking direction and leader affirmation		Are self-managing and self-directed	
Have higher stress levels		Tend to have lower stress levels	
Find tasks are constantly falling between the cracks; "I thought that was someone else's responsibility" is a common cry		Find tasks do not fall between the cracks	
Have heightened frustrations as individuals often find on completion of a task that someone else has done it before them		Minimize the repetition of tasks and wasted effort	
Find overtime and never having enough time are common features of team working		Work less overtime	
Cannot implement performance management and cannot hold individuals accountable		Can implement performance management and define accountably	
Underutilize resources		Optimize utilization of resources	
Find planning and evaluation is hit and miss at best		Can plan and evaluate with accuracy	
Prioritize incoherently, with individuals working to their own agendas		Prioritize effectively	
Can never seem to do enough		Can do more	
Are less effective and struggle to deliver success		Are more effective and ultimately more successful	

This is particularly important when an individual has two homes – a project team home and a functional team home. The following questions will help begin the required discussion:

- Have the roles changed recently or are they relatively static? – New projects, new team remit or is it business as usual?
- Have goals changed such that the previous understanding of roles is no longer valid?
- Is it that people are unclear of their own role, the roles of others or both?
- How often does the team/team leader review goal progress and role changes?
- How often do performance management meetings/reviews occur?
- How do team members reconcile individual work goals and team goals when priorities have to be made? Does this cause role confusion?

Suggested approaches

Role clarity is absolutely a team leader's responsibility. Take time to define the roles and responsibilities of each team member, one-on-one, in delivering team goals and work with them to clarify the links between team goals and team roles for individuals and the team as a whole. Discuss with each member the extent to which they feel they have the skills, equipment, resources and support to deliver on their role. Make sure any identified gaps are addressed through coaching, training or mentoring. Listen carefully to team members; they really do know what they need in order to carry out their jobs effectively. To begin this process there, should be an accurate and up-to-date job description for each team member.

Having completed the individual sessions, it is then essential to hold a team meeting where, in the context of the team goals, each team member describes their role and the way in which their performance is dependent on all other team roles. This should cover role, responsibilities, challenges and support required from colleagues. If there are any changes in the team – personnel or goals – this exercise should be repeated on a regular basis. Use this session to work with the team to produce a map of how each role is integrated with the delivery of the team goals and then sign off with each individual on their own role and responsibilities, standards of performance and deliverables.

Regularly check with each team member how clear they are on their role and the team goals, making sure you clarify roles and emphasize interdependencies. Creating an ongoing discussion in the team on how they can support each other to deliver on the goals is a very proactive means to ensuring collaboration, building trust and creating an environment where asking for help is a good thing and not seen as a negative. This is a big contributor to psychological safety within the team. Provide recognition for support given by one team member to another to reinforce its value to the team.

A lack of role clarity is one of the greatest barriers to team effectiveness. Teams with role clarity are substantially more successful than those without. It takes a team leader to recognize its importance and create the processes to ensure it is an ongoing activity for the team. It's not difficult but takes commitment. You know it makes sense!

A question of morale or motivation?

Role clarification is a prerequisite for motivation. It is about creating the conditions where an individual can exercise their motivation. It is, however, closely linked to goals. Without goal clarity, it is impossible to define role clarity. You cannot establish role clarity without goal clarity. An individual's goals heavily impact their role. This concept touches on all the theories of motivation outlined in Chapter 3. There are two issues at stake in terms of role clarification: the individual's functional role and their team role. In the traditional intact team these are similar, but have subtle differences. In project, virtual and TWG teams these can be substantially different, depending on the purpose of the team and the manner in which the team members have been selected. If an individual is split between a functional role and a project role, the team roles will be considerably different and there will be greater complexity for the individual in managing both roles. This needs support that only the leader can provide. The clarification of roles is without question a leadership responsibility. The leader should check in with team members regularly on their roles and what changes need to be noted, adopted and initiated.

It is all but impossible to exercise motivation if one is not clear on the role. This includes an understanding of the goals of the role in terms of both the individual and the team. McGregor states, "The essential task of management is to arrange the organizational conditions and methods of operation so that people can achieve their own goals best by directing their own efforts toward organizational objectives."[41] Without role and goal clarity, this is not possible.

In his article "One More Time: How Do You Motivate Employees?"[42] Herzberg suggests specific ways in which organizations can develop a programme of what he calls 'job enrichment'. Job enrichment is an attempt to increase the challenge of the job and respond to our need for greater control, autonomy and accountability. Again, this is about role clarity and goals, with both being agreed with the individual.

In their research, Latham and Locke demonstrated that 'challenging' goals impacted motivation in a positive sense – enabling it to be exercised.[43] Their research clearly showed that general goals, easy goals and overly difficult goals had the opposite effect. Without agreed role and goal clarity, motivation will not be exercised by the individual.

Vroom's Expectancy Theory[44] ties in with both Herzberg and McGregor in this regard. This theory tells us that people make associations in terms of expected outcomes and the contribution they feel they can make towards those outcomes. This links with Herzberg's ideas in terms of achievement, work itself and advancement and with Maslow's ideas in terms of esteem, which, yet again, indicates that none of these are possible without role and goal clarity.

Key focus for the team leader: Commit time to both role and goal clarity. Schedule the time required on a regular basis, hold meetings with team members on an individual basis, and then share the output on a team basis. Make sure that each member not only knows what they are expected to do but that they understand the expectations of all other team members. It is important to engage the individual in the discussion and not simply impose. Agreed roles and goals, and importantly agreed routes to their accomplishment, are critical elements to motivation being exercised. Be specific about both and avoid vagueness and generalities that are open to interpretation. Remember that people work best when they can direct their own efforts towards the task and its accomplishment, but that this demands absolute clarity in terms of expectations.

Role clarity is about who does what in the coffee-making process. Who buys the coffee, who maintains the necessary equipment to make a good brew, who makes the coffee, and who ensures the right accoutrements and biscuits are available? There is a lot that needs to be done to get a good cup of coffee and everyone needs to know their function in the process. Otherwise you will get a very ordinary cuppa and probably not one that all team members will accept.

Chapter 10.

Leadership behaviour and participation

Appropriate leadership behaviour

Appropriate Leadership
An ability to inspire and being prepared to do so in a manner suitable to or fitting for a particular purpose, with the intent to maximize the efforts of others towards the achievement of a goal.

> **"Before you are a leader, success is all about growing yourself. When you become a leader, success is all about growing others."**
> Jack Welch

There are many leadership and team models, and all argue for flexibility in leadership style. Some suggest that, as a team evolves, its leadership style should move from a directive style to a delegating style. Others advocate matching leadership style to the experience of team members and their readiness to undertake certain tasks or to enter new phases of a project. Nonetheless, it is generally accepted that flexibility in leadership style is essential and that one style does not fit all circumstances or individuals.

An effective team leader will understand this requirement for flexibility and, in evaluating their own performance, will examine not only the leadership style adopted but also the appropriateness of that style. To evaluate effectively, the leader will need information and feedback from team members. The quality of this information will rely on open dialogue between the leader and team members and on the leader having the confidence to ask the team, "Is there anything I can do to improve my leadership of this team?"

When teams are initially formed, they take on a new project or set of objectives; an effective leader will focus on being directive to ensure that team members understand goals, role outcomes and success criteria. Subsequently, as the team (or project) progresses through its life cycle – and assuming the leader performs the many tasks of leadership appropriately – the team should become more self-managing and self-directing. A directive and controlling style throughout the whole life cycle of a permanent team or project (beyond the initial stages) will not only frustrate a team, it will prevent the growth and development of that team.

Furthermore, a leader must always be aware that, while the team may call for a particular overall leadership style, some individual members may, on occasion, need to experience leadership differently. For example, the delegating style used with experienced and long-serving members may not be appropriate for new members, who will need more direction and support. Meanwhile, in the case of a poorly performing team member, the leader may need to revert to a coaching style with that individual. For a virtual team and a TWG, a different emphasis is required for the leader compared to a collocated traditional or project team. In the virtual team, advanced skills in delegation, fostering shared leadership, goal setting, role clarification, communication and performance management are essential. In the TWG, the larger pool from which a shift is drawn means a greater disparity in individual capabilities, demanding even greater flexibility and awareness from the leader.

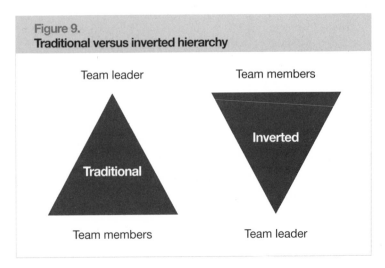

Figure 9.
Traditional versus inverted hierarchy

Team leader | Team members

Inverted

Traditional

Team members | Team leader

Sounds complicated? Not really. In adopting the appropriate style(s), team leaders should perceive themselves as part of an inverted hierarchy. Rather than taking a position at the top of a pyramid and being supported by the team members, they should see themselves at the bottom, supporting the team members and their performance (see **Figure 9**).

In such a position, the management of coaching, performance, goals, communications, upskilling, planning and evaluation becomes the natural task of the leader. This, in turn, leads to the natural adoption of the appropriate style of leadership for the team and its individual team members, helping to drive overall team performance.

The leader's job is to ensure that nothing gets in the way of the team's performance by supplying the strategy and structure for the team to successfully deliver quality, output and customer service. One leadership style does not fit all, and a team leader will have to flex their style to accommodate the team as it evolves. Tasks and power, as well as responsibility, must be delegated to ensure that the team can forge ahead in achieving its goals. How often do we see team members being given responsibility but no power to deliver their responsibility? The leader must possess openness and awareness, as well as flexibility of style, to ensure that the needs of individual team members are met.

Is your team being led with the appropriate style? If the team has the characteristics in the left-hand column of **Table 12** (next page), it may need a change in leadership style.

For a team leader, it is a daily balancing act between over-supervising and under-supervising, each carrying a negative impact. Finding that balance for the team overall and meeting the individual needs of members is a key task of leadership. Remember, it is not the team leader's job to do all the team's tasks; rather, it is to enable and support the team members to deliver.

Table 12.
Team appropriate leadership characteristics

Teams without appropriate leadership	Teams with appropriate leadership
Lack or have misplaced confidence	Display confidence
Constantly seek direction	Are self-managing
Avoid decision making	Have a clear focus
Are fearful of mistakes	Have an appropriate sense of ownership
Have tenuous loyalty at best	Have loyalty to the team leader
Avoid extra effort	Go the extra mile when required
Keep quiet about bad news	Enjoy high levels of trust and openness
Find it difficult to be motivated	Tend to be more motivated
Have a sense of 'flight or fight' and the accompanying stress levels	Experience high morale – will want to belong to the team
Feel frustrated	Feel valued as individuals and as a team
Are constantly threatened by attrition	Have high retention
Tend to have the few carry the many	Have an equitable division of labour
Allow poor performers to 'get away with it', leading to a sense of unfairness	Do not carry poor performers
Are less effective and struggle to deliver success	Are more effective and ultimately more successful

Questions and actions to be addressed by the team and leader

Team leaders cannot make the determination on the best style without engaging with team members. This can be done both on an individual, one-to-one basis and with the team in a group session. It is in fact best done in this sequential manner:

1. Find out what the team expects in terms of leadership by meeting with team members on an individual basis.
2. Establish what is working or what needs to be changed. Collate the views and present them to the team for discussion.
3. Discuss and agree with the team the philosophy of leadership required; for example, more directive, more supportive, more encouragement, more delegation, a mix?
4. Ask yourself as a team leader, "Am I relying on a 'one style fits all' approach?"

Suggested approaches

Consider seeking feedback on your specific behaviours. This is one of the appropriate times to introduce 360-degree feedback and make use of behavioural assessment instruments, such as Belbin,[25] Insights,[26] Myers Briggs,[27] DISC,[28] True Colors,[29] NEO Birkman,[30] Hogan[31] or OPQ.[32] As a leader it is your responsibility to understand yourself and your preferred style and evaluate it for its appropriateness. Discuss the outcomes with your team and commit to listening to feedback. Make the required attempts to change your style and behaviour, always requesting feedback on progress. This is not about removing your prerogative to lead and to manage, nor is it by any means about abdicating your responsibility in these areas. It is about you becoming a better leader, demonstrating emotional intelligence and resilience, and finding the best way to get the most from the team. Always remember that the only way a team leader can be successful is for the team to be successful. You can enable or impede that success through your choice of leadership style. This is about opting to behave in a certain way to meet the identified needs of the team. This is something that is open to anyone.

Keep the team focused on effective leadership practices and ensure the feedback is not personalized. It is essential when having this discussion to encourage effective leadership across the team – it is not all dependent on the team leader. Every team member can provide leadership in the manner in which they perform their role, contribute to team discussions, critique performance (their own and others), innovate and constantly seek better means to continually improve performance.

If you are prepared to have this conversation as a leader (and not all are), you will enhance your team's perceptions of you. If you make feedback on performance a routine within the team, and if you are prepared to seek and embrace feedback aimed at change and improvement in your leadership approach, then all team members will be more accepting of feedback. You will have led by example and potentially created one of the most effective learning platforms possible for the team.

Do not be afraid to seek feedback and support from outside the team to change behaviours and provide monitoring. If you believe that as a leader you need to build leadership skills, find and attend a leadership development programme, sign up for coaching or mentoring programmes if available, or ask other experienced leaders for guidance. Seeking help, development and support in any aspect of your work is not a sign of weakness. It is a sign of maturity and professionalism.

Having said all that, there is only one way to ensure that you are delivering the appropriate style of leadership for your team – you must ask your team members!

A question of morale or motivation?

The leader and their style, attitude and behaviour are some of, if not *the* most, important elements for motivation. Individual team member success delivers overall team success, and this ultimately is the only way the team leader can be successful. The critical elements of this relate to McGregor's Theory Y thinking[41] and the concept of the inverted hierarchy of leadership.

Theory Y leaders believe that people are naturally positive in their attitudes to work. They adopt the attitude that the individual will take ownership of their work, seek and accept responsibility, want to work on their own initiative, and solve problems creatively and with imagination, if allowed.

The inverted hierarchy embraces the principle that for the leader to be successful the team members must be successful. This means accepting the principle that, rather than the team being there to support the leader, the leader is there to support the team. The leader's job is to get everything that impacts or inhibits the team's performance out of the way. The team deliver output, quality and customer satisfaction; the leader is responsible for strategy and structure. This principle links closely to Latham and Locke's Goal Setting Theory[43] in having clear and challenging goals and Vroom's Expectancy Theory[44] in having the right resources available (e.g. equipment, time), having the right skills to do the job and having the necessary support to get the job done (e.g. leader support and correct information on the job). All the foregoing are a leader's responsibility and, if addressed correctly, will create an environment where individuals can exercise their motivation.

Key focus for the team leader: Embrace the inverted hierarchy. In doing so, as a leader you will perceive the challenges of leadership very differently. Pay attention to the issues of morale as in goals, planning, composition and organization (the issues of strategy and structure). Constantly ask yourself, "What can I do to enable my team?" "What is in their way of delivery?" McGregor's Theory Y[41] approach clearly states that team members need to be provided with the resources to do the task and supported in its accomplishment – clearly a function of inverted hierarchical thinking. Always remember that, as a team leader, your team members' success is not only your success but the only way that you can be successful.

There is bad coffee, there is good coffee and then
there is gourmet coffee. So it is with leadership. Which
are you? Anyone can get their hands on the bad coffee
– it's cheap and nasty, readily available, and takes little
or no effort to produce. Good coffee takes time and
effort to produce and gourmet coffee can be difficult
to find and is very expensive. So maybe good is good
enough, but good takes effort. At the very least, you
have to be in the good coffee variety.

Participation

Participation
*The act of sharing in common with another or with others,
embracing consultation in decision making, goal setting and
teamwork to foster or increase team members' commitment to
collective objectives.*

"A genuine leader is not a searcher for
consensus but a molder of consensus."
Martin Luther King, Jr.

Optimal participation in teamwork occurs when team members
contribute, to the best of their abilities and with confidence, to
mutually recognized goals. Success in teamwork centres on achieving team goals and on these achievements being recognized by
the team leader and the organization. Participation is, therefore,
crucial for ensuring team success as it helps to maximize the contribution of everyone in achieving team and organizational goals.

There must be participation by all team members for the
team to succeed. It seems like stating the obvious and most team
leaders when challenged on this issue will respond, "Of course,

all team members participate." Yet it is not uncommon to observe a range of behaviours and dispositions that clearly indicate a lack of participation.

Participation is often taken for granted by team leaders and many teams lack optimal or even adequate levels of participation. Symptoms of poor participation by individual team members are easily recognized by the thinking team leader. They include keeping quiet about bad news, not voicing opinions at meetings, not raising awareness of obvious failings, withholding good ideas, becoming withdrawn, having an excuse for failings, telling the leader what they think the leader wants to hear and low confidence. These characteristics can be observed in the team in general or in individual team members, particularly where some team members are allowed to dominate at the expense of others.

These symptoms will adversely affect a team's chances of being effective and of successfully achieving team goals. Symptoms of poor participation can easily go unnoticed when the team leader does not ensure they are managed and represent a failure of leadership if they are not recognized and acted on. Team members can have many inhibitions and concerns about sharing and participating. A team leader must be aware of this to create a safe psychological environment in which true participation can be realized. In establishing this, a leader should demonstrate humility by acknowledging their own lack of knowledge on some issues and by asking thoughtful questions about challenges that face the team. On this issue, a leader should 'lead from the front' by living the behaviours they are promoting and demonstrating them consistently so that others feel safe in adopting them too.

A leader who conveys an awareness of their own fallibility makes others feel safe in doing so as well. It helps to remove the fear that a team member might have of appearing stupid if they voice an opinion. A safe psychological environment builds trust among team members, improves communication and, most importantly, ensures that the leader hears what needs to be heard and not just what they want to hear. Team members' confidence grows and their sense of value increases as they develop awareness of how much they can contribute to the team. The resulting sense of inclusion and cohesiveness encourages a 'team spirit' while bolstering individual commitment to the team and its goals.

As individuals, we generally learn in private. We attempt a task and either accept or reject the outcome. In a team, an individual is more exposed to the risk of appearing stupid or incompetent when attempting a new task. The fear of embarrassment can prevent a team member from taking a risk. As the feeling of psychological safety develops, the fear of failure among team members lessens and individuals become more open to learning from their mistakes. A safe psychological environment promotes learning, and teams that embrace learning will seek newer, better, faster and more creative ways of doing things. Chapter 3 deals with the issue of psychological safety in more detail. Use **Table 13** to determine if your team enjoys full participation.

There are many quotes one can look to from famous people, writers, academics, management gurus and politicians, all advocating the importance of collaboration and teamwork. All point to the leader as the focal point, but, as retired American professional basketball player, Kareem Abdul-Jabbar, said: "One person can be a crucial ingredient on a team, but one person cannot make a team." All have to participate for the team to be effective. Enabling participation is a key task of team leadership. Are you, as a leader, the key ingredient?

Table 13.
Team participation characteristics

Teams without participation	Teams with participation
Lack confidence	Have confidence
Don't listen but hear what they want to hear	Engender mutual respect
Knock new ideas rather than embrace them	Find new ways to do things
Resist challenges	Rise to the challenges presented
See problems not opportunities	See opportunities not problems
Cannot learn from each other	Learn from each other and with each other
Tend to see the challenge as someone else's problem	Develop shared ownership of the challenges
Are disengaged, withdrawn and even isolated	Feel engaged
Experience little or no personal development	Experience personal development
Can't commit – no means to do so	Are committed
Find the experience a chore	Enjoy working together
Waste effort and lessen efficiencies	Maximize their combined capabilities
Are a group of individuals, not a team	Are truly collaborative
Are less effective and struggle to deliver success	Are effective and ultimately more successful

Questions and actions to be addressed by the team and leader

Participation is dependent on the level of psychological safety that is experienced within the team. Without question, this is a leadership responsibility in creating the conditions for the team. The disposition of the leader and their example, in terms of how they lead, are vital in this regard. I strongly recommend that leaders read the part on psychological safety in Chapter 3 again and then consider the following questions in the context of the team:

- Can team members challenge each other and their leader?
- Do team members openly and regularly ask questions?
- Will team members admit to weakness and seek support?
- Do team members regularly offer new ideas?
- Do some team members dominate team meetings – is there equal air time for all?
- Is the team culture one that hides bad news?
- Do team meetings generally revolve around the leader?
- Are team members' ideas ever appropriated by others?
- Is it easy for all team members to speak up about what is on their mind?
- Are mistakes held against an individual in the team?
- Are team members eager to share information on what does and does not work?
- Is the team inclusive and does it embrace all members without regard to any differences?
- Is it safe to take a risk on the team?
- Is it difficult to ask other members of the team for help?

Suggested approaches

In a team session, ask the team for feedback on how greater involvement and participation could be achieved. Prior to the session, as a team leader, think about the team members in terms of their individual approaches – style versus confidence versus newness versus acquiescence versus don't give a damn. Think about a plan to encourage those who are quiet and to dilute the influence of the overly assertive members, ensuring that everyone gets equal air time.

Be prepared to provide one-to-one coaching as necessary and even consider extending 360-degree feedback to the entire team, opening the opportunity to discuss styles at a team meeting. Always seek to understand why an individual is not participating. Is it because they are new to the team and lack confidence? Are they naturally shy or introverted? Do they just need encouragement? Are they being dominated into quietness? Watch out for passive/aggressive behaviour within the team and stamp it out immediately, if it is apparent.

Adopt a consultative approach wherever possible and seek the support of more senior and long-term members as appropriate, to encourage all to participate. This is where any team member can exhibit leadership, ensuring that their colleagues are given air time and have their opinions actively sought in all discussions.

Examine ways to increase the empowerment of team members – consider how team members could grow by being given more responsibility and provide them with uninterrupted time to report and present on their areas of responsibility during team meetings. Help the less participative gain confidence in this manner and let them experience others hearing and valuing their input.

Seek and listen to feedback from team members and, as a leader, become more active in seeking consultation and input into decisions. Never allow a situation to develop where asking questions appears ignorant and challenging the status quo appears negative. If there is bad news to be heard, you as the team leader need to hear sooner rather than later and never, as in some cases, not at all.

With the team, identify projects in the work programme that the team could manage with minimal input from the leader or where other team members could lead and be recognized for that leadership. Regularly ask each team member what issues they are facing in their role and what additional support they require.

Psychological safety is an essential element for participation. The sense of a psychologically safe environment is wholly dependent on the team leader.

A question of morale or motivation?

Motivation is not possible without participation. A key responsibility of the team leader is to ensure that all team members participate to the fullest of their individual capability. If motivation is a choice made by individuals, then their full participation is essential for motivation to happen. Encouraging participation requires understanding of the differing requirement of all team members. It requires flexing the leadership style to meet these differences. The astute leader will recognize that no one style of leadership fits all. Some team members work best with direction and need it. Maybe they are new to the team, or more junior and upskilling as they come to terms with new tasks. Some are experienced campaigners and require a delegation style of leadership. Some are more than capable but don't realize it and need encouragement.

The degree of participation of team members is directly related to the style of leadership and the attention placed on this critical issue by leaders. Participation is crucial for ensuring team success (and thereby leader success) as it helps to maximize the contribution of everyone in achieving team and organizational goals. Essential to this equation is the need to recognize poor participation and continually address it.

The traits of poor participation overlap with many of the traits associated with poor psychological safety. In many regards, these are clear indicators of a lack of motivation being exercised by team members. This is an issue directly related to Maslow's ideas and the 'esteem needs' of individuals. Maslow argues that people are not born apathetic but that their inability to meet esteem needs makes them so.[45] Feeling unsafe, being afraid to speak up, and being ridiculed for raising ideas and questions are guaranteed to undermine the self-esteem of team members. A failure to create a psychologically safe environment that provides a platform for participation is not only a failure of leadership; it is a wanton waste of intellectual capital and company resources. These symptoms, if present, will adversely affect a team's chances of being effective and of successfully achieving team goals.

Key focus for the team leader: Consider and understand each team member and the appropriate style of leadership they require. Ask your team members what they want from you in terms of leadership and then deliver it. Focus on the issues of psychological safety and ensure that everyone feels confident to express opinions, give bad news (if necessary), is not afraid to ask questions for fear of ridicule and that all team members are given equal air time. People are naturally motivated to do a good job. How many people do you know who get out of bed in the morning and think to themselves, "I am going into work today to do a bad job"? So, when team members are not performing, and are obviously not experiencing morale and not exercising motivation, the likelihood is that it is the organization or team leader that is failing and not the individual. To quote Shakespeare, "The fault, dear Brutus, is not in our stars. But in ourselves." Take this sentiment as your starting point in addressing these issues.

Caffeine is a central nervous system stimulant and participation is the caffeine of the team world. It is what gets the team moving and keeps it working. It creates the conditions for team members to exercise their motivation and ensures that all members can contribute to their fullest, keeping everyone engaged.

Chapter 11.

Commitment and communication

Commitment

> **Commitment**
> *A strong belief in an idea or system and a willingness to give your time and energy to something that you believe in. Team commitment is the individual's psychological attachment to the team.*

> **"The greater the loyalty of a group toward the group, the greater is the motivation among the members to achieve the goals of the group, and the greater the probability that the group will achieve its goals."**
> Rensis Likert

Commitment to the team can cover a broad array of concepts, from the willingness to give all for the sake of the team to sacrificing individual needs to the needs of the team and the mission. Commitment to the team and each other can be evidenced in the degree to which team members feel they can depend on each other. Commitment and trust are wholly intertwined. Truly high-performing teams are those where members have confidence in each other's words and deeds. They are committed to each other.

None of us should underestimate the importance of commitment within the team – that sense of just knowing team members can be relied upon. Many teams never fully get there. There is always a lingering doubt about the level of commitment from some individuals or the team as a whole.

When the stakes are high, the requirement for confidence and trust in the team escalates. For the team of climbers tackling Mount Everest or firefighters entering a burning building, knowing that your team can be totally relied upon is essential. While in the workplace the stakes may not always be so high, the benefits of a committed team still matter and still enhance performance.

Commitment should have a label on it that reads, 'Fragile: Handle with Care'. Achieving a level of trust and a sense of reliability within a team not only takes time but also requires lots of consistent good practices. The feeling of confidence will grow over time if the team consistently delivers for each other. One event can damage this confidence. Once that sense of trust is broken, it can take a significant effort to rebuild it and, in some cases, it may never be regained.

Reliability results from some fundamental practices and behaviours within the team. Understanding the mission and aligned goals in the same way, truly knowing the roles and responsibilities of each team member, and coordinating and integrating the individual efforts in keeping with the team plan are some of the practices that form the basis for trust. Building a climate within the team of respect through honest, open communication, holding each other to account and not shying away from difficult conversations are some of the behaviours that support the maintenance of team commitment.

As the team establishes a pattern of delivering to each other, it becomes the norm, and, as members demonstrate it more and more to each other, it becomes less likely that someone will consistently ignore this norm. Instead, team members may feel morally obliged to conform and meet the often unspoken expectations of delivering on their promises. It can become a virtuous cycle and soon it is just 'the way we do things'.

Team leaders play a critical role in ensuring this pattern is embedded in the team culture. They achieve this through standard good practice regarding the establishment and clarification of goals and roles. They recognize their behaviour will be crucial in setting the tone within the team. They highlight how important it is for the team to rely on each other and codify this in the team's operating principles. They acknowledge and reward examples of commitment early in the team's life and frequently as the team develops. They discourage team members from giving the answers the leader would like to hear.

Team leaders ensure that, like team goals, the promises made are not aspirational efforts, but genuine commitments to deliver. They encourage feedback within the team and look for specific examples of members demonstrating commitment and loyalty. They do not ignore the need to address poor performance, whether it is in terms of tasks or behaviours.

Table 14.
Team commitment characteristics

Teams without commitment	Teams with commitment
Lack confidence in the team	Have confidence in each other to deliver
Splinter and form cliques	Are united and cohesive
Do not deal with conflict appropriately	Manage conflict effectively
Are guarded in their communication	Are open and honest
View leadership as ineffectual	Consider the leader as effective
Are more stressed than other teams	Are more focused than other teams
Avoid feedback	Seek feedback
Repeat their mistakes	Learn from the past
Misunderstand roles and responsibilities	Understand roles and responsibilities
Have a blame culture	Recognize contributions from others
Do not deliver on promises	Do not promise unless they can deliver
Achieve less	Go the extra mile
Find it hard to trust	Trust each other
Are less effective and struggle to deliver success	Are more effective and ultimately more successful

Leaders also know that, as the team evolves over time, the levels of commitment will grow but don't become complacent about it. When membership changes, effective team leaders do not trust osmosis to ensure that this sense of trust will transfer to new members. They proactively ensure that it happens. They know that confidence based on commitment has been achieved through good practice and they consciously articulate and reinforce the message: "This is how we do things."

Which of the characteristics in **Table 14** (on the previous page) apply to your team? Are the team members committed? The characteristics in the right-hand column are available to all teams with effort. What does your team need to address and improve?

Questions and actions to be addressed by the team and leader

Commitment cannot be left to chance. As with all aspects of the effective team, the issues surrounding commitment need to be addressed by the team in a group setting. These questions are a good place to start in a team discussion on commitment:

- Has the team created a culture of not wanting to say 'no' to each other?
- Does the team make promises to deliver when the reality is that it is are unlikely to do so?
- Do team members, not the leader, hold each other accountable for failing to deliver?
- Does the team have a set of agreed operating principles? If so, has it identified delivering on its promises as a key principle?
- Are there any challenges of remote working impacting on the team?
- Are there any multicultural factors at play?
- Are there any skills gaps impinging on effectiveness or efficiency?

Suggested approaches

Have a team discussion on what reliability looks like for the team – for examples, look at where it is working and where it is not working. Reliability cannot be assessed without agreed performance standards and performance measures in the team. The first order of business is to ensure that there are agreed goals and objectives and that team members know what success and achievement look like. Then it is possible to consider the issue of reliability in terms of individual performance, achievement and people doing what they said they would do. Make sure all team members are clear on the interdependencies in the team and the importance of meeting quality standards and deadlines.

Monitor workloads and performance standards as the leader, but also ensure that team members are engaged in assessing performance and holding each other to the agreed standards. Tackle non-performance and provide individual feedback to team members who are not performing to the standard required. Feedback is essential to keep everyone on track. You will be surprised how often someone thinks they are doing what they should be doing only to find out through feedback that they are not. Conversely, make sure that recognition is provided to team members who are demonstrating the reliability and dependability required.

In a team session, develop a charter on how the team operates, and use this as a standard for how team members are expected to behave. This is the issue of operating principles. It is all very well to develop these principles, but where most teams fall down in this regard is in the failure to agree sanctions for breaches of the principles. There must be consequences if a team member fails to live up to agreed principles.

Seek input from individuals on what they see as undermining trust in the team and what would help to build trust. Think about the following statement on a scale of 1 to 7: "Team members fully trust each other in this team." A response of 1 indicates no trust and 7 full trust. A good approach to discussing trust in the team is to present the team with the statement and ask them to discuss what would have to happen for the team to score a 7? The resulting conversation will quickly inform the team about what behaviours are impacting them, what needs to change, and what is hampering the development and sustainability of trust among team members.

Having faith in one's colleagues is the hallmark of an effective team that consistently delivers. It is not just a matter of good fortune in the assembled membership. It is the result of consistent practices and behaviours reinforced over time, initially by the leader and subsequently by the team.

A question of morale or motivation?

Commitment is about the ability and readiness of team members to rely on each other and it is very much a question of motivation with a liberal sprinkling of morale. Commitment is something an individual will make when they consider it appropriate and safe to do so. You cannot make an individual commit with all that it entails. You can lead a horse to water but you can't make it drink.

Commitment is a concept that cannot be isolated and dealt with directly. It happens because the more tangible issues of morale and motivation are in place. The concept of commitment depends on a number of issues – common purpose, enthusiasm, confidence in the future and, most importantly, loyalty. All matter in generating commitment and all are concerned with morale. Equally, leadership behaviour and leadership participation that encourage a psychologically safe environment are critical, which are issues of motivation. Team members must feel psychologically safe in order to display commitment and to be able to rely upon and trust each other.

Commitment must have a label that reads: 'Fragile: Handle with Care'. Achieving a level of trust and a sense of reliability within the team not only takes time, but lots of consistent good practices.

Key focus for the team leader: Consistency in approach is essential. A focus on the issues of psychological safety in the team, ensuring that people can speak up, are heard, are not ridiculed for their ideas or treated dismissively when they ask questions, are all critical to psychological safety and, ultimately, commitment. Misappropriation of ideas must also never happen. Nothing breaks trust and commitment as quickly as a team member's ideas being appropriated by someone else in the team as their own.

Ensure that the issues of morale are addressed and pay attention to the issues of leadership and role clarification and commitment. When this is done, trust will build and be maintained in the team. Commitment is one of those things that matters for motivation to be exercised but cannot be addressed directly. It can only be established and maintained through the consistency of approach described in the other key focus areas of morale and motivation (see Chapter 3).

Commitment is like the water we use to make the coffee. If it is always fresh, it will make good coffee – as long as it is decent coffee in the first place. If it is sitting in the pot for too long, if it has been contaminated or if it is drawn from the hot tap and not the cold tap, the resulting brew can be so awful it will leave a bad taste and can even put people off coffee altogether. Once broken, commitment based on trust can leave an equally bad taste and damage the team beyond repair – it can put people off the idea of the team completely.

Communication

> ### Communication
> *A process of reaching common understanding, in which participants exchange information, news, ideas and feelings to create and share meaning. The word communication comes from the Latin* communicare, *which literally means 'to share'.*

> **"When the trust account is high, communication is easy, instant, and effective."**
> Stephen R. Covey

Honest communication may sometimes be painful but it leads to greater effectiveness in the long run.

When there are relationship or performance problems in working teams, members will often single out 'communication' as the root cause – almost as if communication were some disembodied force (for good or evil) over which they have no control.

Symptoms such as dissatisfaction with the perceived blunt style of a top-down leader or the lack of information sharing on a project are attributed to this 'ungovernable' force rather than to the plain fact that communication policy in the team or organization is unheeded, ineffective, misunderstood or simply non-existent.

Communication is a broad term with a range of context-specific definitions. So, it is important that there is a common understanding of what the concept actually means and how it is understood by each team member, both in the context of what they are attempting to achieve and in advance of developing and adopting a communication policy and procedures.

In rescue teams involved in life-or-death situations, where precise and effective communication is critical, operating procedures tend to highlight very specific needs. Standard terminology when communicating information is essential to avoid confusion, as is ensuring statements are direct and unambiguous. Rescue teams appreciate the need to communicate all information required by those external to the team, informing the appropriate individuals when the mission or plans change. They agree a range of methods of nonverbal communication as appropriate and establish the means to request and provide clarification as needed. They use a defined order when communicating information and stick to it. All of the above is to ensure as little confusion and misinterpretation as possible, recognizing the critical role communication plays in saving someone's life. These procedures do not happen by accident, nor do they evolve out of simply having time spent together. They are carefully thought through and, once agreed, are accepted by all on the team and implemented rigorously.

Many teams do develop appropriate means for communication similar to those described above. However, they can fail to consider the degree to which team members feel that communication is honest.

Honest communication is where team members feel free to say what they think or 'tell it like it is', believe they are being listened to and heeded, are not punished for reporting bad news and have regular forums for open information exchange.

Open and honest communication about what team members think and feel is critical. If team members do not fully believe their colleagues are open and honest in 'telling it like it is', then relationships and effectiveness can easily be undermined. Meanwhile, uncertainty and suspicion will impact the trust within the team, and the effective integration and coordination of team tasks is likely to result in a failure. The formation of cliques characterized by sniping and blaming behaviour quickly follows, with people only telling each other what they think others want to hear. An increasing tendency will emerge to avoid challenging discussions that relate to performance issues or to address the conflicts naturally occurring in any team. This can lead to team members feeling isolated or ignored and a drop in levels of commitment and effort.

The leader has a significant role to play in supporting the development of honest communication. There is a need to recognize that communication is not just about sharing facts and information. For honesty to prevail, team members need to trust each other implicitly and establish policies and practices to support honest communication.

When teams form initially, communication may be guarded and reticent. Members will be testing the parameters, observing the operating styles and adhering to the communication norms being established consciously or unconsciously by the leader or informal leaders. This is the ideal time for leaders to role-model open and honest communication.

As the team matures and develops, levels of trust will change. If the team rewards honest communication over time, members will learn that this is a valued element of the team's culture. If honesty is not encouraged, or if it is punished, then team members will not take the risk of being open and honest.

The traditional intact team, whose members meet face to face, can communicate with more ease than other team types. Virtual teams, dependent on electronic modes of communication, need to develop very robust communication processes, nearly as rigid as those of the rescue team, described previously. Highly diverse teams with various cultures and languages and the TWG, with its ever-changing membership, present very different challenges for team leaders seeking to implement communication procedures. Team leaders who can rise to these challenges will be in a far better position to optimize their team's effectiveness than those who don't.

Communication for the team is so important that any one of the characteristics in the left-hand column of **Table 15** can have a very negative impact on overall effectiveness. Carefully consider this table and identify if any of the negative characteristics are a reality in your team.

Table 15.
Team communication characteristics

Teams without communication	Teams with communication
Withhold information selectively	Share information freely
Avoid giving or seeking feedback	Continuously provide and seek feedback
Do not trust their team colleagues	Implicitly trust their team
Do not deal well with conflict	Manage conflict effectively
Repeat mistakes	Learn from their mistakes
Can splinter into cliques	Feel united as a single team
Miss deadlines	Deliver on time
Can be unclear about their roles	Are clear on their roles and responsibilities
Are unaware of their weaknesses	Know their strengths and weaknesses
Feel stressed	Feel in control
Feel undervalued	Feel valued
Fail to innovate	Are willing to try new ways
Tolerate poor performers	Manage performance effectively
Are ineffective and struggle to deliver success	Are effective and ultimately more successful than other teams

Questions and actions to be addressed by the team and leader

The word 'communication' originates from the concept of sharing. If a team is to effectively develop working and appropriate communication protocols, they must share their opinions and feelings on communication. Again, this is a situation where the team leader should address these issues in a series of one-to-ones with team members, collate the information and then initiate a group discussion. It is of paramount importance to protect everyone in the formulation stage of a communication strategy for the team. The one-to-ones may well elicit some very direct criticisms of individuals. This must be anonymized before presentation to the group. Once an agreed communication strategy is in place, there should then be an expectation that members will call each other out on breaches. Consider the following questions and use them as a guide to both the one-to-ones and the group session:

- Why are people feeling that team members are not completely honest in their communication?
- Are people selective in what they say to the detriment of the team?
- Do people agree to things despite having reservations?
- Does the team leader demonstrate and role-model openness and honesty?
- Are team members shunned or punished for their honesty? Is it perceived as negativity?
- Do people feel that team members deliberately retain information as it can be a source of power?
- Are team members suspicious of each other?

Suggested approaches

Make sure all team members are clear on the interdependencies within the team and the importance of timely, appropriate and honest communications. Have a team discussion on what honest communication looks like for the team – look for examples of where it is in evidence and where it is not.

Agree how the team can assess the extent to which there is honesty in communication and agree on certain benchmarks. Provide individual feedback to team members who are not performing to the standard required. Take time to review communication structures and messages across the team to pick up on behaviours that could be a cause of concern. Review and define with the team what the formal and informal communication processes will be.

Address honesty and appropriateness of communication in a team charter on how the team operates and use this as a standard on how team members are expected to behave. Seek input from individuals on what is blocking communication in the team and what would help to build trust.

Do not be afraid to directly challenge misinformation when it is verbalized by team members. This should cover issues of concern to the team itself as well as the rest of the organization. At the end of the day, this could be a disciplinary issue.

Hold regular team meetings and generate discussion on topics in dispute. This will allow the team to generate a common understanding and misinformation can be challenged. In times of high instability or change, increase the regularity of team communication sessions.

Communication within teams is essential for effectiveness. However, it is not simply the mode or style of communication, or the frequency or content that team leaders should concern themselves with, but first and foremost the degree of honesty.

If people are open and honest, then they can truthfully say that meetings are ineffective or effective, that there is too much reliance on email or not, or that there are not enough one-to-one conversations or too many. From the outset, team leaders need to encourage team members to be confident and speak their minds.

A question of morale or motivation?

Good communication drives enthusiasm within a team and enthusiasm is a question of morale. Enthusiasm is a product of mission clarity, confidence in the future, loyalty and, most importantly, communication within the team. If a team is unclear about its mission and purpose (communication dependent), and lacks confidence in the future, it is unreasonable to expect the team to exhibit enthusiasm. One needs a purpose, a focus and a route to do something to become enthusiastic. Appreciation by the team and the organization as to the value of what the team does is also a precondition for genuine enthusiasm to be experienced. Constant and appropriate communication within the team and from outside the team in terms of stakeholders, is of paramount importance to ensure that enthusiasm, once engendered, is maintained. Enthusiasm and confidence are intertwined but are driven by good communication and undermined by poor communication. It is hard to be enthusiastic without confidence in the future and, likewise, it is hard to have confidence in the future without enthusiasm; neither are possible without communication.

Key focus for the team leader: Communication and more communication is the key to maintaining enthusiasm within a team, assuming the other issues of morale are being correctly dealt with. Team leaders must ensure that the flow of information within the team, and between the team and the organization, is appropriate in terms of providing feedback and recognition for the team. Whether the team is off or on target, the feedback loop through communication is what serves to maintain enthusiasm for the job of the team. Whether this is to correct what is wrong, get back on target or build on existing success, all serve to support and maintain enthusiasm. The leader who listens to team members' ideas, innovations, questions and concerns will also support the maintenance of enthusiasm.

Ensure that team members' attributes and skills are understood. Allocate roles and responsibilities to members that maximize the return for the group. Coach where required, support new members in the early days and don't leave their assimilation to chance. Develop weaker members to where they are fully contributing and enlist the help of stronger or longer-term members to support this endeavour.

Leaders have to recognize that appropriate sharing of information, efficient channels of communication, and frequent meetings or conference calls, to make sure that everyone – everyone – is up to date, are critical aspects of communication within teams. The reliability, quality, openness and honesty of that communication is equally important.

Communication is the coffee filter of the team world. Three things matter for the coffee filter: strength, or it will tear or rupture; capacity, in its ability to hold the coffee grounds and still allow flow; and efficiency, in terms of the particle sizes it will remove. Of course, you need the right filter for the right coffee maker. Team communication is similar. It needs to be strong, it needs to get the right stuff through to the team with the right flow (timing), and each team needs the communication that is right for them.

Chapter 12.

Planning and evaluation

Planning

> **Planning**
> *The process of deciding in detail how to do something before you actually start to do it; a fundamental property of intelligent behaviour.*

> **"By failing to prepare, you prepare to fail."**
> Benjamin Franklin

It's not just about having a plan – it's about planning.

Despite the plethora of tools and techniques now available to teams, planning is consistently identified by team members as an 'issue' impacting on performance. Teams, reflecting the work styles and personalities of individual members, can often be addicted to action. The need to get things done and quickly move towards the goal can undermine the need to systematically plan. The result of this action orientation can have an impact not just on efficient task accomplishment but also on the relationships within the team.

However, it does need to be acknowledged that, in some organizations, very sophisticated planning practices and policies exist to which teams are obliged to adhere. While in general terms these practices ensure planning is consistently undertaken, teams may find that the methodology is not necessarily the most appropriate for the project or work at hand. Teams can over-plan. They can end up investing time, effort and energy in developing plans, reports and critical path analysis that the work simply does not warrant.

Teams need to be conscious of the potential negative impacts of both under-planning and over-planning. Appropriateness is the key and leaders need to encourage early conversations to discuss what planning is needed to deliver the goals.

Planning as a process not only maximizes the potential for a smooth and efficient route to goal accomplishment but also helps clarify the shared understanding of these goals; it ensures team members are clear in their roles and have a better sense of other members' roles. All team members can appreciate where the team is heading and, critically, where the work scheme or project is now, versus where it should be.

Planning is a future-oriented activity, helping to align the work of team members, co-ordinate and integrate their separate contributions, and allocate the required resources and equipment. When the planning practice is appropriate to the goals, team members can feel more confident about what they are doing, both individually and collectively. Equally, it generates a sense of the team being organized and that the leader is ensuring the infrastructure is in place to give the team the relevant roadmap.

Without appropriate planning, teams struggle. The team may actually achieve the goals, despite the lack of effective planning, but the unnecessary frustration, inferior quality outputs, re-working, confusion, unseen risks, customer dissatisfaction, and damaged team or team leader reputation can be the cost. This can result in conflict, significantly undermining a team member's commitment to the team or team members.

Planning is not just a process of identifying tasks, establishing logical sequencing, exploring risks, allocating resources, managing dependencies, and developing charts and reports. Planning is also, critically, the platform for reflection through evaluation. As a team considers its status in terms of the plan, it is engaging, understanding what went right and, more importantly, what went wrong. This reflection gives the team the opportunity to innovate and improve its processes, including its planning process.

The application of best-practice planning methodologies will help the team consider all these aspects of its work, and provide an agenda for communication between team members and reporting to external stakeholders. Appropriate planning is a critical tool in developing and enhancing the team's *esprit de corps*.

It builds confidence in individuals, between team members and their leader, and sustains their sense of managed control.

Does your team have the appropriate planning techniques in place? There is no one best way. For some teams, a Monday morning review is sufficient, while others may require the deployment of advanced software and all that goes with it. Each team must determine what is right for them. Regardless of whether sophisticated or basic planning in needed, the characteristics in **Table 16** apply. Check your team's current status against the table and determine what you need to do.

Table 16.
Team planning characteristics

Teams without planning	Teams with planning
Are disorganized	Are focused and achievement-oriented
Are inefficient	Utilize all their resources appropriately
Develop high levels of stress	Displays a calmness and capability
Experience conflict and frustration	Enjoy better relationships
Waste time	Manage time effectively
Tend to achieve less than other teams	Can go the extra mile when required
Have nothing to evaluate	Can adjust effort as required
Experience high levels of staff turnover	Are perceived as an achieving team within and without
Regularly see tasks fall between the cracks	Allocate tasks appropriately
Blame each other when problems arise	See problems as a collective responsibility
Struggle with performance management	Can recognize each other's contributions
Lack leadership	Have a sense of control and security
Lack confidence in each other	Are more committed to each other
Are less effective and struggle to deliver successful outcomes	Are more effective and ultimately more successful

The existence of a plan is not planning. When the team engages with the appropriate planning process for its goals, it maximizes the potential for achievement and the generation of a high-performing team culture.

Questions and actions to be addressed by the team and leader

I regularly ask teams if they have appropriate planning in place. Very often I will hear the response, "We are not sure what you mean by the question." This is a clear indication that there is no planning in place, which means there also cannot be any effective evaluation going on. The team must have a plan, otherwise they cannot possibly know where they are or what they are doing, and evaluation of any progress is meaningless. You have to have something to evaluate. The team members must contribute if they are to truly work for and deliver any plan. The following questions are not an exhaustive list, but they represent a good place to start a planning discussion:

- Do team members have different expectations about what good planning looks like?
- Are some team members more action-oriented and find planning a waste of time?
- Are some members uncomfortable without having every aspect of the work thoroughly planned, when that may not be necessary?
- What is the leader's approach to planning?
- Have the team been provided with the necessary tools and knowledge for effective planning?
- Have the goals changed recently or is the strategy emerging rather than clearly defined?

Suggested approaches

Take time with the team to identify what is currently working well in relation to planning and what the areas for improvement are. Agree on an appropriate, systematic approach to planning. Remember that different tasks, depending on complexity and duration, require different levels of planning.

Ensure team goals and targets are clearly driving the planning cycle for the team. Individuals who hold both a functional role and a project role can often confuse the two and this, in turn, can impact the planning process. It is conceivable that any given team can have multiple plans in place at any given time, and that an individual team member can be involved in multiple teams, adding even a greater number of constraints to the planning process. Also keep in mind that the teams may have to carry out activities such as budgeting separately to satisfy the organization's needs rather than the team's needs.

Ensure there is a mechanism to continuously review activity against the plan. This adds life and meaning to any plan. I see many teams plan but never review the plan until they reach the end of the project. This is simply planning for planning's sake. The plan is a living thing, designed to help the team on an ongoing basis and, therefore, must be subject to ongoing review.

Where there is a high level of complexity and interdependency among the team tasks, advanced planning techniques may be required. Seek help if this is not a skill set of the team. Many organizations have a cadre of project planners whose very job is to help plan and manage complexity in delivery. Advanced planning is a skill set that many team leaders and team members do not have, so do not be afraid or reluctant to seek support. The more complex the project, the more critical the planning requirement. That said, where there is a dearth of planning skills within a team, the leader should take steps to develop these skills among team members.

The use of an external specialist to help draw up a team plan can be particularly advantageous if there are a lot of emotive issues within the team with regard to the work to be done. This of course might also be indicative of other team issues, such as a lack of clarity on goals and roles, and may indeed reflect on the psychological safety of the team environment.

Resistance to planning and monitoring can result from team members not understanding the value of plans for work programmes and resources. This should be made clear to the team.

For people to believe in the value of planning exercises, there needs to be ongoing review and realignment. Otherwise, it could feel like planning for planning's sake.

A question of morale or motivation?

Planning is closely related to confidence in the future, which, in turn, relates to the mission of teams and the overall environment in which a team exists. Confidence in the future is a key aspect of morale.

Is the mission relatable? Is it achievable? Is it challenging and interesting for the team members? Good planning goes a long way towards clarifying these issues for team members. Will it sustain the team over time (the operational period) and does it have real meaning for the organization overall? Is what the team doing important to the organization and is it recognized by the organization? Nothing undermines morale more than a lack of confidence in the future. Without planning, how can an individual know what the future may look like and, indeed, if they are doing the right things to protect their future.

Being achievable and relatable are important attributes for any team mission. If the team members do not believe it can be achieved, their confidence will immediately be undermined. Remember the old maxim – whether you believe you can or you can't, you're right!

Planning is critical in this context. Teams are task-oriented. They want to jump into action and 'do' things. Good planning, taking the time to understand where you need to go as a team, and identifying the key milestones on the way that will inform the team of their achievements are all critical in terms of team confidence.

Key focus for the team leader: Regularly reinforce the team vision and mission, and ensure that all team members and new joiners fully understand it. Broadcast the team's mission to other teams and engage with other team leaders where there is interaction and interdependency, ensuring that those around the team understand the team's challenge. These are critical tasks that precede planning for a specific task or project. In reporting team output against a plan, show recognition for a team member's input and contributions using the individual's name, and ensure their recognition by the organization. If there is change happening around the team, focus on understanding that change, communicate it with the team and adjust the plan as required. Even when the future is unclear, keep a dialogue going with the team in terms of what you know and strive to remove uncertainty as much as possible. In a vacuum, when there is a lack of communication, team members will fill the void with the rumour machine. This is seldom accurate and can severely undermine confidence.

Always ensure that planning remains high on the team agenda, that it involves all team members, and that it is regularly revisited and updated.

A good cup of coffee in the morning sets you up for the day and can change your view of the world, providing stimulus and energy. Planning sets the team up for the task or tasks at hand and changes the team's perspective on the world, providing them with direction and confidence.

Evaluation

Evaluation

The primary purpose of evaluation, in addition to gaining insight into prior or existing initiatives, is to enable reflection and assist in the identification of future change.

"True genius resides in the capacity for evaluation of uncertain, hazardous, and conflicting information."
Winston Churchill

Where are we? Where should we be?

The headlong rush by teams to deliver can create the impression of enthusiasm, passion and commitment. Observers can remark on the team's focus, energy and determination. Team members can revel in the sense of purpose, action and progress. These are important but can equally become issues that, ultimately, undermine team performance and team relationships. In essence, the rush to deliver can become team 'mindlessness'.

Evaluation in a team context is critical to ensuring ongoing team success. There is a direct link with team goals which cascade into the team's planning process through to evaluation.

However, evaluation is not just a phase of the planning methodology. It also requires the team to evaluate 'what' is being done, 'why' it is being done and 'how' it is being done. This 'how' refers as much to the teamwork of the group as it does to the activities required to achieve the task – does this sound familiar to some previous comments in earlier chapters?

All team members should have the information and knowledge to understand and indeed accurately explain where the team currently is, in terms of its plan. This necessitates understanding the overall team goals, the roles and responsibilities of the team members, and the step-by-step sequence of tasks and activities required to deliver. The more effectively the team adopts relevant planning practices, the easier evaluation can be accomplished. Teams need to factor in evaluation sessions into their plans. When do we take stock of where we are and where we should be? What information do we need to help us accurately gauge progress and risks? Some teams and team leaders adopt these practices unconsciously and they become part and parcel of team review meetings and one-to-one conversations. For many teams, these practices have to become a conscious dimension of how they work together.

A focus on action can deflect the team from reflection on where they are and where they should be. This is ultimately to the detriment of the team's overall goal.

However, there is a further dimension to evaluation above and beyond the reporting of progress against the plan. This aspect of evaluation relates to questioning, such as – why are we doing this? Is there a better way to achieve the goals? What have we learned so far? How are we working together as a team? How can we be better?

Team evaluation can become overly focused on the task and the issues relating to the activity, and not on some of these fundamental questions. Teams can have superb, state-of-the art plans, but unless they allow space and time to evaluate the rationale for what they are doing or how they are collaborating as a team, the evaluation aspect can be considered only half-completed.

Teams need to factor in critical evaluation on a regular basis. The regularity and frequency will vary considerably from team to team, but it should be planned in. In particular, teams that have had a relatively consistent membership over a long period should take time out to evaluate and reconsider their *raison d'être.* Have any team activities become fossilized and redundant but are still adhered to? An example may be the Monday morning meeting. It is not that the purpose of the team has changed or that the customary practices are automatically obsolete, but that teams should consistently question what they do and how they do it.

Table 17. Team evaluation characteristics		
Teams without evaluation	**Teams with evaluation**	
Don't know where they are	Know precisely how they are progressing	
Are caught by surprise	Anticipate risks and deal with them	
Miss deadlines	Adjust to ensure timely delivery	
Make mistakes	Learn and innovate from problems	
Can become stale and reactive	Are dynamic and proactive	
Are unable to prioritize	Maintain a clear and appropriate focus	
Don't question	Perceive different opinions as constructive	
Engage in activity for activity's sake	Focus on results-driven action	
Are erratic in delivery	Are consistent in delivery	
Have high levels of stress	Experience less stress than other teams	
Have a blame culture	Hold each other accountable	
Lack confidence in each other	Trust and understand each other's roles	
Question the leader's abilities	Trust the leader	
Are less effective and struggle to deliver success	Are more effective and ultimately more successful	

In discussing and evaluating the answers, it may be concluded that all is well and no changes are needed for now – but this is an essential ongoing conversation. There are many negative characteristics associated with the team that fails to evaluate. Consider **Table 17** and determine if your team has a healthy evaluation process.

Questions and actions to be addressed by the team and leader

In my opinion, most people do not have in-built evaluation skills. These are skills acquired through one's working life and with experience. As has been pointed out, evaluation is a more comprehensive process than simply reviewing a plan and encompasses not just 'what' is being done but also 'how' it is being done. The following questions should be considered by every team leader individually and together with the team in a group session – evaluating how we evaluate!

* Do the team appreciate the value of evaluation?
* Do the team and team leader understand the need to evaluate both what has been achieved and how it has been achieved by the team?
* Does evaluation focus exclusively on results and key performance metrics?
* Are there any similar patterns of concern with the team's planning? Without planning, evaluation is not possible!
* Are the team evaluating the 'how' as well as the 'what'?
* Does the team have an appropriate and team-recognized means of evaluation?

Suggested approaches

With the team, identify what is currently working well in relation to evaluation and what the areas for improvement are; agree a systematic approach to evaluation that is appropriate for team tasks. Ensure team goals and targets are clearly driving the planning and evaluation cycle for the team. Team members have to be clear about the use of evaluation information and that its purpose is to improve team performance and not single out individuals for public criticism. Using the evaluation methodology to call out poor performers in front of their peers will not create a healthy environment or encourage team members to fully participate in the evaluation process. If the evaluation process is indicating individual performance issues, the leader should deal with this on a one-to-one basis. As a team matures, and its confidence and commitment develops, team members will naturally address non- or poor-performance with colleagues directly.

At a team session, brainstorm the most appropriate measures to evaluate the team's output. Consider the use of external information, e.g. customer satisfaction levels, as part of evaluating the team's performance. Research what is out there in terms of quality and evaluation methodologies to identify the best approach for the team, building the evaluation method most appropriate for your team. It takes time to establish evaluation expertise and there is a certain degree of trial and error, which is why, as explained previously, these are skills that are acquired over time.

As part of any evaluation process, teams need to consistently reflect on and discuss how they are functioning together as a team. Are there any issues impacting the team's effectiveness? Have roles changed or do they need to change? Are there skills missing that need to be developed? Issues impacting team members must be dealt with sooner rather than later. Otherwise they will fester and potentially prove harmful to relationships and inhibit the delivery of goals. Remember, it is not just about the plan, but about how we execute the plan together.

A question of morale or motivation?

Without accurate information and understanding of where one is and where one needs to get to, it is almost impossible to expect an individual to exercise their motivation. All team members should have the information and knowledge to understand and, indeed, accurately explain where the team currently sits in terms of its plan. This must become a conscious dimension of how team members work together. They have to work hard at getting the principles of evaluation established and these should be thought of as 'part of the way we do things around here'.

The impact of evaluation on motivation cannot be underestimated. Unfortunately, it is not an area that teams do particularly well. All the motivation theories discussed and referenced in this book infer (or at least imply) the need for sound and appropriate evaluation. To direct one's efforts towards goals (McGregor),[41] one needs to know and understand progress. To meet safety needs (Maslow),[45] one should avoid capricious decision making and receive reliable information on progress. For advancement, recognition (Herzberg),[42] and expectancy (Vroom),[44] are all to a greater or lesser extent impacted by evaluation. Ultimately, goal attainment (Latham and Locke)[43] is dependent on evaluation. If you do not know where you are going, how do you know where you are supposed to be?

Key focus for the team leader: Working with the team determines the most appropriate means of evaluation for the team and their tasks and goals. This varies considerably from team to team and is wholly task dependent. For some it is a regular weekly progress review meeting and for others it can be the deployment of advanced project planning software and all the training that goes with it. It is a case of what is appropriate. Once the means is determined, it is critical that evaluation takes place on a regular basis. This will allow for adjustments to be made when the team is off course and for recognition to take place when the team is achieving.

Reflective time for the team is also critical and this should be scheduled on a quarterly basis as a minimum. There must be time for the team, away from the day-to-day operational issues, to discuss their *modus operandi* as a team. Do we understand goals in the same way? Are we clear on our roles and are we using our combined skills? Are we dealing with the differences in performance? Is our conflict management style working for us and delivering innovation rather than further relationship issues? Is there anything we want the leader to do differently? Is our planning and evaluation appropriate? This is, as always, about addressing the 12 criteria of team effectiveness as needed.

Evaluation is the coffee tasting or 'coffee cupping'
of the team world. Coffee cupping is a practice
performed by professionals known as 'Q Graders'.
It involves the coffee taster attempting to measure
aspects of the coffee's taste, specifically the body,
sweetness, acidity, flavour, aftertaste and bean origin.
This practice aims to fully understand and grade a
bean. Team evaluation is no different!

Chapter 13.

Recognition and conflict

Recognition

> "It is an immutable law in business that words are words, explanations are explanations, promises are promises – but only performance is reality."
> Harold S. Geneen

Recognition of team members by leaders, in acknowledgement of them having reached specific goals or achieved high-quality results, is meant to encourage repetition, through reinforcing the behaviour one would like to see. We all tend to be fairly good at this aspect of recognition. The challenge comes when the behaviour we recognize is one we do not wish to see repeated and this is where many team leaders fall down. When I say recognition, I mean the recognition of good, bad and average performance equally and dealing with them.

The failure to recognize and deal with the differences between good, average and poor performance is one of the greatest demotivators and is without any ambiguity a leadership responsibility.

The better you are at what you do, the more work you are given and the less support you receive, while the converse is true of the poorer performer. How often is this situation a reality in many organizations and teams? In some respects, it is understandable. On a Friday evening with a crisis developing for a customer, who does the busy leader give the problem to?

Unfortunately, this is too often the scenario when a team must perform a critical task. The workload is unevenly distributed,

the better performers are overloaded and the poorer performers
are underutilized. If this is an ongoing situation, it will have a
number of consequences.

When one talks about recognition, the automatic assumption
is that it is about acknowledging good performers, saying thank
you and even offering rewards such as bonuses. Recognition
means acknowledging all levels of performance and dealing with
them. The leader who only recognizes good performance and
ignores poor performance creates an interesting dynamic in terms
of performance standards.

This is a subconscious dynamic or effect that is seldom articulated and, once instigated, is very difficult to stop. When poorer
performers are allowed to 'get away with it', the impact for the rest
of the team is the subconscious lowering of performance standards
to the lowest sanctionable level. The extra effort required to deliver
in terms of the recognition received is not worth it. In fact, the
unfair distribution of workload leads a high performer to believe
that they are being punished for being good at what they do.

The lowering of performance standards is but one consequence.
Team members who have to carry poorer performers, and observe
the team leader not dealing with this issue, develop a number of
emotional responses, in terms of both the leader and other team
members. Again, these are not necessarily articulated but, nonetheless, impact on team members' dispositions.

They may consider the leader as ineffectual in this area and,
by extension, can come to believe that the leader is ineffectual in
other areas. This leads to issues relating to loyalty and belief in the
leader. Relationships between the good performers and the poor
performers can become fractious, impacting on team cohesiveness.
On the one hand, the situation is unfair to the good performer
as they have to carry a greater workload. On the other hand, it
is also unfair to the poor performer, who is not being supported
to improve. In many cases, the poor performer is unaware of
their poor performance and does not understand that they need
to improve or, indeed, specifically what they need to improve.

The poor performer can become isolated and develop feelings of exclusion, which can become only too real and spark off a whole new set of dynamics, including claims of bullying.

Performance standards and equitable workloads are not only essential in terms of fairness, equity and team spirit; they are indubitably a baseline for team effectiveness. No team can maximize its effectiveness without equitable performance standards. This is a leadership responsibility.

This is not just an issue of performance management and regular formal and informal feedback, which are the principal tools to be used, but links directly to many of the other responsibilities of team leadership; including goal clarity, role clarity, appropriate leadership style, ensuring participation, communication and conflict management – in fact, all the essential elements of an effective team. Effective performance management is not possible without these other elements, and an effective team is not possible without performance recognition and the ability to deal with recognition on an ongoing basis.

Team leaders must recognize the differences between performance standards and deal with them. Not only are they the person in the team with the power to do so, it is an obligation and imperative of team leadership. To fail to do this is to fail in the role of a team leader.

Does your team have any of the characteristics of a team without recognition? If so, they must be addressed as a matter of urgency. Check your team status against **Table 18**.

Table 18. Team recognition characteristics		
Teams without recognition		**Teams with recognition**
Suffer low morale		Are motivated
Find it difficult to foster team spirit		Display good team spirit
Duplicate effort and tasks fall through the cracks		Maximize their resources
Have minimal innovation		Exist in a learning environment
Find it difficult to rely on each other		Enjoy high levels of trust
Lack a united effort		Are focused on team goals
Struggle with deadlines		Deliver high productivity
Tend to work in isolation		Are supportive of each other
Work to the lowest sanctionable level		Will go the extra mile
Are less engaged		Feel supported by their leader
Have stifled and broken communication		Engage in open and honest communication
Work to what they believe is the priority		Know their role and what they are doing
Tend to allow conflict to become personalized		Manage conflict more effectively
Are less effective and struggle to deliver success		Are effective and ultimately more successful

Questions and actions to be addressed by the team and leader

Whether or not you are using a formal performance management system, or even if you as a team leader are not the person ultimately responsible for an individual's formal performance management (often the case in project teams), you must provide performance feedback to team members – that is, feedback in terms of good, average and poor performance. Performance feedback is never an easy subject, but it is a core skill of leadership. In my experience, people want feedback, and the more immediate and regular the better. If it is not a strong point for you as a leader, get help within your organization from other leaders. You could also seek a mentor on the subject or read up about it and develop the skill. An inability to provide effective feedback will seriously impact both the individual and the team in terms of performance. Use the questions below to begin your thinking about this critical element. As always, take it to a group discussion and agree with the team how it will be managed:

- Does the team have a culture of only recognizing good performance?
- Has recognition of poor performance been left to the leader instead of it being a team responsibility?
- Does the team, team leader and organization as a whole have an aversion to dealing with poor performers?
- Are poor performers left to do whatever minimum contribution they make while good performers are punished with more work?
- Does the team define what good, average and poor performance look like?
- Does the team leader role-model and encourage upward feedback on their own performance?

Suggested approaches

Use team meetings to discuss how people would like to see improvements in the level of recognition in the team. Identify what it is people perceive when they consider that performance levels are inconsistent and encourage team members to hold each other to account. Review the issues from Chapter 11 on commitment and think about whether team members deem each other reliable and trustworthy.

Use a range of methods to recognize the contribution of team members. This can often be down to small things, such as saying 'thank you' more often. But it can be overdone as well, where positive acknowledgement becomes trite and loses its impact. Always remember it is never just about positive feedback. The issues of poor performance being recognized and dealt with are of paramount importance. It is a comparative concept. If all that is ever provided is positive feedback, what value does it have if team members see poorer performers continually getting away with it? It is all a matter of balance and, as said previously, giving feedback is a skill to be learned and developed.

Publicize outside the team where team members have made significant contributions and ensure that there is acknowledgement and recognition for the individual. Identify what organizational processes are available that can be used to provide recognition to the team and team members. Increase the level of overall recognition within the team. Encourage team members to provide recognition to each other for work well done and make sure that recognition mechanisms do not inadvertently reward low standards or poor performance. Consider innovative options in terms of recognition – feedback from peers can be very motivating. Additionally, you should consider how leading specific projects or occupying high visibility roles would give appropriate recognition to certain individuals.

Be aware that individuals have different personal preferences in terms of recognition and motivation. Tailor recognition to personal preferences where possible. Acknowledge where organizational processes, such as salary reviews, militate against the team pulling together (e.g. rewarding individual performance over team performance). I know it sounds complicated, and it is, but it is vital if team members are to exercise their motivation and true potential.

Failing to deliver performance recognition is to waste time, money and resources and serves to demotivate team members and undermine morale. It does take time and effort and team leaders need to develop the skills to manage performance. It is a transformational style of leadership that works through insight and vision and guides team members towards the goal.

A question of morale or motivation?

The failure to recognize and deal with the differences between good, average and poor performance is one of the greatest demotivators. If there is one area of focus for a team leader that has the most impact, I would suggest it is this issue of recognition. It links to all previous elements described and to the issues of morale. It is clearly linked to the motivational theories in every respect (see the section in Chapter 3 on morale and motivation). Performance recognition is a critical element of each of the following:

- Vroom[44] – the concept of instrumentality, in terms of a clear understanding of the relationship between performance and outcomes, is not possible without good recognition practices.
- Latham and Locke[43] – Goal-Setting Theory critically depends on feedback as a means to encourage the exercise of motivation.
- Herzberg[42] – counts recognition as one of five key motivators.
- Maslow[45] – esteem needs are dependent on high self-esteem and the esteem of others, which includes recognition by others.

The impact for a leader in this area is far-reaching. A failure to deal with recognition undermines a team's belief in the leader and their leadership of all other areas in the team. When belief in the leader is undermined, morale (that sense of wanting to belong) is undermined. With morale under threat, motivation will not be exercised – unless, of course, it is the motivation to move jobs. Feeling undervalued and punished while others coast along often sees a team experience high levels of attrition. It is often the better performers who leave. Why would the poorer performer leave and take the risk of gaining a new leader who might actually make them work?

Key focus for the team leader: Ensure that you have regular performance discussions with each team member. This does not have to be a formal 'performance review'. It is about checking in with members to ensure their tasks and goals are on track. In the true spirit of the inverted hierarchy, it is about asking if there is anything you can do to help. Is there anything in their way? You want your team members to succeed, they want to succeed, and their success is the only way you, as a leader, can succeed.

In order to manage feedback effectively, think about the demands of the millennials (see Chapter 1), who seek coaching and not supervision, peer structures, and opportunities to interact with many peers and leaders rather than being limited to a single leader or traditional small team, all of which can aid multi-source feedback. They want a leader working within the group setting, rather than instructing from a distance. Being collocated means more opportunities for regular, informal feedback. Feedback in real time, little and often, is what is demanded. This immediacy of feedback demand is best met by weekly conversations, be that via chat forums, team video conferences or face-to-face meetings. Millennials want meaningful interpersonal work relationships and the regular informal check-in is a critical element of this. This is possible in a teaming culture with leaders collocated with their teams in an open and collaborative environment. The traditional manager-subordinate approach does not accommodate this type of communication.

> Recognition of the various attributes of different coffees, and the various ways it can be made and served, is what delivers the best coffee for each of our tastes. Recognizing and managing team behaviours, and the differences between good, average and poor performance, as well as individual capacities, is what delivers the best for each of our teams.

Conflict

> ### Conflict
> *An active disagreement between individuals or between groups; a state of opposition between ideas, interests and opinions, creating friction and disharmony.*

"Conflict is inevitable, but combat is optional."
Max Lucado

Whether conflict is harmful or beneficial, ultimately, it is due to the manner in which it is dealt with.

Conflict has many definitions, including a state of war, a state of opposition between ideas, disagreement, controversy or simply a clash between two appointment times, e.g. a diary conflict. It can also be referred to as discord, strife, contention or dissension. In psychology, the term 'to be conflicted' may be applied to having two simultaneous but incompatible wishes, which sometimes lead to a state of emotional tension.

In the context of a team, conflict generally means a difference of opinion on how something should be done, who should do it or even what should be done. Differing values, objectives, perceptions and expectations among team members can all lead to conflict.

Depending on how this conflict is addressed by the team – and the leader in particular – it can have negative outcomes, such as the aforementioned discord and strife, as well as stress, anxiety and reduced productivity. Conflict can also have positive outcomes that lead to increased productivity, more efficient processes or product and service innovation.

All forms of conflict have the potential to become personalized. Where emotions are substituted for work issues, blame, anger and frustration take the place of problem solving. More often than not, the result is lost productivity.

In dealing with conflict, and in order to encourage positive outcomes, it is helpful to know its source. Team-based conflict tends to emanate from four principal sources.

Task conflict arises when people are performing non-routine tasks that differ on approach and priority. This is typical in a new team or a project team that has just been assembled.

The conflict centres on tasks rather than personal issues and so it tends not to lead to (inter)personal conflict. Such conflict can be a positive phenomenon, introducing a healthy debate among peers that, in turn, leads to the team identifying the most agreeable way forward. In reaching agreement, individual views, opinions and approaches are explored and, in most instances, a better solution is arrived at based on a combination of individual inputs. Task conflict is often worked out by the team members themselves and, once resolved, tends to hold.

Process conflict arises over operating procedures, rules of engagement and the roles assigned to team members; it is a feature of established teams. It centres not on the task itself but on how the task is managed.

This type of conflict centres on processes as opposed to personal issues. While in theory it should not lead to interpersonal conflict, it is more likely to do so than task conflict if not addressed promptly. Achieving a positive outcome from process conflict is more likely to require the intervention of a leader than in the case of task conflict. And, as with task conflict, once agreement is reached it tends to hold.

Organizational conflict arises when team members perceive or experience inequality or ambiguity. It is likely to arise in teams where the goals of individuals differ from those of the team and where there are status differences between team members and differing reward systems. It can also arise where there is competition among members for scarce resources.

Organizational conflict, featuring inequality and unchecked competition among team members, inevitably leads to interpersonal conflict where suspicion and mistrust are rife, and a multiplicity of agendas impacts the attainment of team goals. This tends to be more pronounced in recently formed project teams and TWGs, and less so in traditional teams.

Social conflict is associated with poor team leadership when symptoms include over-controlling leadership, stifled discussion, unevenly allocated tasks, unproductive meetings, over-dependency on a few and obvious favouritism. Social conflict is a characteristic of an unsafe psychological environment.

Social conflict results in dissatisfaction, misunderstandings, poor communication, feelings of unfairness, isolation and exclusion. Such conflict combined with (typically) overbearing leadership absorbs creative energy and stifles innovation.

Pre-emptive strategies for dealing with conflict include establishing agreed team operating principles, with a clear statement on how conflict will be handled and a set of standards for communication between team members. This, in turn, requires regular checks on how well such an agreement is holding up. Within the check-ups there are opportunities to amend the agreement to suit the evolution of relationships, which will be a feature of any team as it matures.

While personality differences are an easy throwaway explanation for team conflict issues, there is still the fact that individual personality styles can irritate or annoy team members. This can be accentuated in teams with diverse cultural compositions. Establishing a set of operating principles, minimizing opportunities for the sources of conflict described and maximizing opportunities for people to develop good positive interpersonal relations, will help mitigate conflict.

Most importantly, a team leader must create a safe psychological environment where team members feel valued and feel free to express their views and concerns, knowing that they will be taken seriously.

Conflict is normal and natural in teams. It should not be avoided. It must be addressed or it will fester. It is the ultimate source of innovation in a team. Debate and differences of opinion generate new ideas and new ways of doing things – what is to be avoided? As I have said previously, conflict is not a problem, only the way we manage it.

A leader needs to be able to identify the types of conflict that are likely to become problematic. They should have an understanding of the sources and nature of the conflict and be efficient in devising creative alternatives, compromises and solutions for reaching agreement and finding the most productive way forward.

A leader must also recognize and be satisfied with the fact that not all conflicts can be resolved to everyone's satisfaction. It is okay to agree to disagree when this is the only option, although this should be a rare event. The leader is the one who should then make the decision on the way forward, explaining their rationale for doing so. It's why the leader is the leader!

Conflict, when managed well, will deliver innovation. However, intense conflict distracts people from the task at hand, because of the harmful emotional state that it creates. Leaders are the only ones in the team with the power to ensure that appropriate conflict management techniques are in place. This is a key task of leadership. Conflict around routine tasks and conflict that is allowed to become relationship conflict (personalized) are failures of team leadership and the leader. See how your team measures up against **Table 19**.

Table 19.
Team conflict characteristics

Teams without conflict management	Teams with conflict management
Suffer poor interpersonal relations	Enjoy a positive environment
Often appear irrational and out of control	Approach conflict in a rational and reasoned manner
Find problems a barrier to performance	Use differences of opinion as opportunities
Cannot see the wood for the trees	Continuously innovate
Struggle with routine tasks	Always have time to tackle new tasks
Have little or no trust among members	Depend upon and trust each other
Struggle with new challenges	Welcome a break from routine as exciting
Develop a blame culture	Recognize each other's contributions
Do not allow members to participate fully	Are eager to engage with ideas
Suffer higher levels of attrition	Benefit from high levels of retention
Exhibit frustration and stress	Direct their energy to the goal
Exist in an unsafe psychological environment	Encourage the sharing of ideas and opinions
Lose faith in the leader	Enjoy good leadership
Are less effective and struggle to deliver success	Are effective and ultimately more successful

Questions and actions to be addressed by the team and leader

Thomas and Kilmann (1974)[46] identified five basic ways in which we respond to conflict: competing, accommodating, avoiding, collaborating and compromising. All five are available to us as responses, but we tend to have a preferred or built-in response. A single response to all conflict situations is not a good thing. As with leadership style, everyone needs to flex depending on the situation and both the nature and importance of the conflict. In developing a progressive means to handle conflict within a group, one not only has to understand the overall team disposition to conflict but, ideally, understand the preferred styles of those who make up the team. A good place to start is to address the questions below:

- Does the team shy away from differences?
- Does the team feel conflict is a negative reflection on them?
- Does the team know the range of conflict sources in the team or organization?
- Are the team trained in conflict management?
- Are there behavioural styles accentuating the naturally occurring conflict?
- Are team roles contributing to the existence of conflict?

Suggested approaches

Hold a team discussion on what types of conflict exist in the team. Explore the pros and cons of conflict and look for examples of where it is evident and where it is not. Encourage the team to express differences openly, so they can be discussed and resolved.

Reinforce to team members that they should raise any issue that is causing them concern and bring it to the attention of the leader or to the team in a group session.

Get the team to look at their styles in managing conflict, learn to appreciate other styles and be more flexible in their approach to conflict management. Deploy Thomas and Kilmann's modes of conflict instrument,[46] which helps individuals to understand the nature of conflict and their own reaction to it. It is a very useful approach to generating an informed discussion within the team, leading to an agreed strategy for the team.

As in all discussions, and particularly in a discussion on conflict, ensure that team discussions are not dominated by one or two 'loud voices' without other team members having an adequate opportunity to contribute.

Build awareness of the value of conflict in the team – encourage better problem-solving, greater creativity and innovation by implementing a review process at the end of team meetings. For example, get everyone to individually identify one thing that worked well for them at that meeting and one thing they would like to see improved. Make sure ideas are always treated with respect and acknowledged, even if not acted upon.

Sit down with team members who are not getting on with each other and agree how they will behave with each other – demonstrating dignity and respect at all times and stressing the importance of co-operating to achieve team goals. Reinforce team and organizational goals as the common agenda everyone must work around. You cannot make everyone like each other, but in a team and organizational context we have to have respect that allows all individuals to work to their fullest capacity.

A question of morale or motivation?

The manner in which conflict is managed within a team is a question of morale. Properly managed conflict underpins a sense of loyalty and to be loyal is to demonstrate firm and consistent support and allegiance to a person or institution or, in this instance, to the team. This is one of the pillars of morale and a sense of wanting to belong. This is a mutual concern and issue for the team. Not only must there be loyalty to the team, there must also be loyalty among team members. A belief in a common purpose is important for loyalty to be exercised, as is confidence in the future and, indeed, a degree of enthusiasm for the team and its purpose.

Importantly for the team, the quality of relationships also matters in this element. How the team deals with conflict, seeks resolutions to challenges and differences of opinion, and respects each other are all elements of loyalty in the team. Teams need to establish rules of engagement and need to honour those rules once established. Poor working relationships undermine any sense of loyalty very quickly. Establishing a clear and unambiguous means of dealing with conflict in the team is critical. Conflict should never be perceived as a negative. It is a source of innovation, as differences of opinion are generated and discussed and the best route forward agreed. Conflict between members is not the issue; rather, how we manage conflict is what creates the negativity associated with conflict.

Key focus for the team leader: In consultation with the team, build a set of rules of engagement. Make sure that they are agreed and are appropriate. All members must abide by the agreed rules, which will vary greatly from team to team. Five or six rules are the norm and it is also important to consider sanctions for those who do not abide by the rules. Protect relationships between team members. Do not allow aggressive or passive aggressive behaviour within the team. Call it out when it is apparent. Banning aggressive behaviour might well be a rule of engagement for the team. Ensure that all members get their say at meetings and that some do not dominate at the expense of others. This can mean supporting the more introverted or less experienced members of the team to be heard and to find their feet in the team. Do not allow ideas to be stolen; give credit and recognition to everyone for their ideas and contribution.

"I don't have a problem with caffeine. I have a problem
without it," is a famous coffee quip. Similarly for the
team, what hope have they to innovate, find better
ways to do things, or address problems and failures
without conflict? Conflict is not the problem; it's what
you do with it that determines if it is a problem or not.
You should not have a problem with conflict; it is when
you do not have it that you have a problem.

Chapter 14.

Composition and organization

Composition

> **Composition**
> *The way in which an item's various parts are put together and arranged; a thing composed of various elements.*

**"The strength of the team is each individual member.
The strength of each member is the team."**
Phil Jackson

A well-balanced team means knowing the strengths of each member and plugging the gaps.

There is a well-known phrase in architecture that 'form follows function'. In other words, one does not put up a building and then decide what it will be used for. You do not build a multi-storey car park and then try to put it to use as a hospital!

In the composition of teams, 'function' relates to the goals or purpose of the team and 'form' to the number of members and the skills and abilities of those members. One has to know what the purpose of the team is before one can determine the composition of the team.

It may seem like stating the obvious, but team composition is something that should never be ignored and regularly reviewed. It is surprising the extent to which team members will not even agree on who comprises the team – as in, who the team members are. A survey of more than 100 senior executive teams saw fewer than 10% agree as to who was actually on their team.[13] This phenomenon is particularly common in virtual teams (a growing feature in many organizations), where 'membership creep' can literally push the team to the point of paralysis.

The team composition should always be considered in terms of the goals of the team. The skills and attributes required are determined against this backdrop. Without a clear purpose, the composition cannot be determined. How often does the team leader take time to consider the configuration of the team? As the goals of a team change, it is critical to reconsider the team composition in terms of new goals. Some may need to leave the team and new members may be required.

It is not just about the skills that the team needs but also about the attributes of the individual team members. The degree of heterogeneity or homogeneity can have an impact on the performance of the team. Diversity can be a source of innovation and energy but can also to lead to more conflict. Team members with similar characteristics will tend to be more cohesive, but may lack the missing ingredients to maximize performance. Research at the London Business School (2007)[47] identified that a gender balance of 50:50 led to the most innovative teams. A team leader needs to be aware and cognizant of the degree of diversity in their team and how increased or decreased diversity might impact performance. A group's collective intelligence is not strongly correlated with average intelligence or maximum intelligence of group members. It is more so with social sensitivity, equality in the distribution of conversational turn taking and the gender split in the group.[48] Worth thinking about, I suggest. The composition of the team has implications not only for how the team will perform but also for how the team is led and what constitutes the most appropriate style of leadership.

Team size is also an important consideration. Empirical evidence suggests that the optimal team size is between five and ten members.[10, 11, 12] Teams bigger than this, more often than not, are two or more teams rather than a single team. A common mistake is to consider a department as a team when it is in fact made up of multiple teams, each with their own leadership and purpose and, therefore, each with their own challenges. The larger a team becomes, the more difficult it becomes to achieve focus and manage the relationships and interdependencies between members. Failure to manage these relationships and interdependencies (and they grow exponentially with each additional member) is often the peril upon which the team fails (see the section on team size in Chapter 3). Establish which characteristics are apparent in your team from **Table 20**. If any of the left-hand-side issues are prevalent, you may need to consider the composition of the team, in whole or in part.

Table 20.
Team composition characteristics

Teams with inappropriate composition	Teams with appropriate composition
Lack cohesion	Deliver with focus
Struggle with communication	Develop effective communication internally and externally
Do not know if they have the skills to meet goals	Understand their skills gaps and can plan to close them
Appear disorganized	Can plan and prioritize
Constantly miss deadlines	Expect to deliver on time
Work more overtime	Have the time to do things right the first time
Suffer higher attrition, further impacting configuration	Have higher retention and, because they stay together, perform better
Have increased stress levels	Enjoy good morale
Are less likely to meet expectations of themselves and their customers	Tend to exceed expectations
Cannot determine appropriate leadership style	Will have higher levels of trust among team members
Lack innovation	Drive each other to seek better ways
Make more mistakes and are less likely to learn from them	Learn from their mistakes and openly talk about them
Cannot develop mutual accountability	Expect each other to perform and hold each other accountable
Are less effective and struggle to deliver success	Are more effective and ultimately more successful

An inappropriately configured team cannot effectively deliver what is required of it. On the one hand, a team may have the necessary balance and composition for successful completion of a project and not realize it. On the other hand, it may not have the necessary skills at all and not realize that either! It is only in taking time to consider the team composition that these concerns can be addressed.

Questions and actions to be addressed by the team and leader

In looking at team composition, there are a series of questions for the team leader to answer and there is a separate list of questions that the team should discuss together.

Team leader:

- Am I leading one team or multiple teams as if they were one team?
- Who is actually on this team?
- Does this team have the skills to deliver the purpose or goals of the team?
- Are the right people on this team?
- Do I need to get rid of someone and/or find new members?
- Is the team heterogeneous or homogeneous and am I leading it appropriately?

Team members:

- Have goals changed recently and is the team concerned about its ability to deliver?
- Have new processes been introduced but insufficient training provided?
- Have team members left and been replaced by less experienced or less skilled resources?
- Is there a consistent, development programme for continuous upskilling and training *in situ*?
- Is the team still seeking new members and therefore under-resourced?
- Do the team members collectively believe that they have all the necessary skill sets to support goal achievement?

- Having the skills required is not a static position. Is the team thinking about what skills will be needed in the near and longer-term future?
- Is the leader making sure these will be available to the team?
- At times individuals may be highly skilled but the team as a unit may not capitalize on this, and so lose confidence in its effectiveness. Is the team utilizing all the skills of its members as appropriate?

Suggested approaches

Carry out a review of the skills needed to deliver on the goals of the team and match them to the current skills in the team. Provide training, coaching and mentoring to close skill gaps. In addressing the gaps, agree development plans with each team member – taking account of behavioural as well as task demands.

Where there is a radical shift in the goals or purpose of the team, new tasks, additional responsibility or functionality, the composition must be considered in terms of its ability to deliver. This may mean recruiting new members or changing the team composition to include individuals with the required skills. This is never easy, particularly when loyalty has been developed and a leader feels morally compromised in making the required changes. Nonetheless, there will be times when this is necessary and, unfortunately, sentimentality must be put aside if re-skilling quickly is not an option. In 2002, the *Harvard Business Review* published an article titled "Why Entrepreneurs Don't Scale".[49] A primary reason quoted was too much loyalty to the original team. Once past the entrepreneurial phase, different skills and different attitudes were required and the entrepreneurs who failed could not see past their sentimental feelings towards their original team members. A salutary lesson indeed, with the ultimate price.

Introduce a formal induction process for new team members, whereby more experienced team members coach and mentor them. Do not rely on the organizational induction process alone. Even if an existing employee is transferred into your team,

adopt an approach as if your team is an organization in its own
right (which it is, by the way) and run their induction to your
team with that attitude.

If a particular skill is identified as missing, you may be able to
source it from within the organization short term, until a team
member can be upskilled. Get support in terms of expertise from
the rest of the organization. If there are specific tasks that need
professional skills, co-opt a person on a part-time basis – do not
be afraid to ask and do not wait too long to do so.

Get the team to identify how to keep its skills up to date, in
order to meet requirements and encourage cross-skilling within
the team. Increase flexibility of skills usage between members by
encouraging people to try new ways of working.

If, with changing goals or team remit, there is no option in
terms of changes to team composition, leaders may have to 'cut
their cloth according to their measure'. This can include rene-
gotiating the overall purpose and goals with the organization.
The goals for the team may not be achievable with the current
composition so, instead of setting out to win the championship
(unlikely), the goal might be to avoid relegation.

A question of morale or motivation?

Composition is driven by mission clarity and is a question of
morale. Team members need to be reassured that they have the
right skills within the team to have confidence in the future and
in their combined ability to deliver. Loyalty to the team is also
impacted by composition. If a team member does not feel that
the team is right or does not have a real chance of succeeding,
it is difficult to engender loyalty, which in the end is a pillar of
morale and relates to that sense of wanting to belong. Equally,
enthusiasm, another element of morale, can be undermined
by unsuitable composition. It is hard to be enthusiastic about a
project or goal if one does not believe the wherewithal is present to achieve the required tasks. One needs a purpose, a focus,
a route and the means to do something to become enthusiastic.

Enthusiasm is unquestionably linked to the belief that the team has the skills required to do the job.

Key focus for the team leader: Ensure that team members' attributes and skills are understood. Allocate members roles and responsibilities to maximize the return for the group. Where team members feel that a number of co-workers are not capable of delivering at the required level, there is every potential for more capable members to feel punished for taking on more. The concept of recognition, as raised in Chapter 13, now becomes critical for the team leader to manage.

Coach where required, support new members in the early days and don't leave their assimilation to chance. Develop weaker members into fully contributing team members. Enlist the help of stronger and longer-term team members to support in this endeavour. Carry out a role clarification exercise with the team. Get each member to say what they bring to the team, what they need from each team member to do their role and what they believe their strengths are. Encourage them to discuss what skills they have that are either not being used or that their team members do not know about, what they consider their weaknesses are and where they need help. This is a powerful exercise that can have a major impact on the team and the utilization of all team skills. It is a challenging task that ideally should be facilitated by a strong external facilitator when it is undertaken the first time.

To create a truly great cup of coffee, there are three key points. First is knowing what type of bean species you are purchasing, second is understanding your beans' origin and its effect on flavour, and third is learning about the different roasts and their effects on the overall taste of your brew. You need a similar understanding of your team to get the composition right. What are the skills each member brings (type of coffee bean)? What is their experience and how can they contribute (effect on flavour)? And, by combining their skills, what will be the impact (different roasts)?

Organization

Organization
*The way in which the elements of a whole are arranged —
the structuring of a group of people who work together in
a particular way for a shared purpose.*

"The way a team plays as a whole determines its
success. You may have the greatest bunch of individual
stars in the world, but if they don't play together,
the club won't be worth a dime."
Babe Ruth

I am talking here about organization as the verb and not the noun.
There is stress with disorganization and there is also a cost to
being disorganized.

There is no one right answer to the concept of organization in
teams. What works for one team will not automatically work for
another. Much depends on the purpose of the team, the degree of
interdependency within the team to get the job done, the size of
the team and the location of the team (one or multiple locations).
To deliver the most effective organization for a team, a leader
must not only consider the foregoing but must also assess the
competency, maturity, capacity and dependency of the individual
team members. This links directly to appropriate team leadership
behaviour, and leadership and participation (see Chapter 10).

The organization of a team relates to the management methods
they develop to control not just the work that they do but how
they communicate, how they evaluate and how they plan. It is
also dependent on the veracity of their processes in goal setting
and role clarification.

When team members are asked about organization, there can be
a wide and varied range of responses regarding what concerns them.

In some instances, a well-run weekly meeting confirms for team members that the team is well organized. In other instances, it can become more complicated with teams requiring the creation of sub-groups to handle the work in order for the team to feel organized.

Geographical location can have a major impact on the team and their perceptions of organization. A virtual team requires a clear set of procedures to maintain effective communication, taking into consideration time differences, diversity issues, etc.

The sense of organization in a team is invariably tied up with how team members perceive the sense of direction of the team (goals); how relevant meetings are in terms of informing them (communication and participation) and maintaining an understanding of progress or otherwise (planning and evaluation); how well work is subdivided and allocated (roles and composition); how well conflict and differences of opinion are handled (conflict); and, ultimately, whether the team view the management of performance as a key element of organization (recognition). When team members are carrying poor performers and workloads become unfairly distributed, the team senses disorder and can even question each other's commitment.

In effect, organization touches on all of the elements of team effectiveness. It is not about command and control. It is about the team in discussion determining the most appropriate management practices for their situation, their goals and tasks, their interdependencies. It is about finding the right processes together that can deliver the most efficient manner for the team to work together and deliver. The team's organization must be constantly under review. Processes established for the delivery of one goal can be ineffectual for another. The team needs to adopt an organic approach, evolving their management, control and organizational practices to meet their needs and continue to do so as the team matures.

The astute leader will not impose organization; rather they will engage with the team to understand what works best and will always be vigilant for obsolescence in the team's way of doing things. However, it is a leader's responsibility to ensure

that the team is organized in the most effective manner. The
leader will be blamed by the team where disorganization reigns.

How well organized is your team? Consider the characteristics
in **Table 21** and make adjustments as appropriate.

Table 21. Team organization characteristics	
Teams with inappropriate organization	**Teams with appropriate organization**
Never seem sure of themselves	Act with confidence
Make tasks harder than they are	Make complicated tasks look easy
Do not display a united front	Have a shared sense of direction
Do not see problems when they should	Recognize problems early and deal with them
Do not appear to be in control	Are less stressed and appear calm
Tend to carry poor performers	Enjoy greater equity of effort
Are less sensitive to each other's needs	Recognize each other's constraints
Have higher absenteeism and turnover	Are more stable and suffer less attrition
Struggle to manage performance	Can manage performance effectively
Rarely deliver on time	Deliver on time
Cannot fully utilize their resources	Utilize their resources more fully
Demotivate members	Create the conditions for motivation
Communicate ineffectually	Are engaged
Are less effective and struggle to deliver success	Are more effective and ultimately more successful

As with all elements of team effectiveness, organization is critical. A well-organized team makes complicated tasks look easy. It comprises the right people with the right skills, calmly and confidently doing the right job in an environment that promotes productivity and efficiency. Morale in such teams tends to be high and conditions exist for motivation to be exercised.

Questions and actions to be addressed by the team and leader

Organization should never be imposed but should be arrived at through consensus. This requires an ongoing consultative and engagement process with the team led by the leader. At no point when recommending consultative approaches do I suggest that a leader's prerogative or responsibility is being undermined. The leader has to make the final decisions. The effective leader will embrace engagement and seek buy-in to decisions. Team members who are part of a decision-making process will always be more willing to implement and live by a decision they were part of determining. The following questions will help to start a group conversation on organization:

- What are the specific challenges to this team from an operational perspective?
- Are they a virtual team based globally and across different time zones?
- Are they based in different parts of the same site or office?
- Are they a TWG with constantly changing membership and the organizational challenges this can bring?
- Do team members use indicators such as team documentation or team meetings to determine how organized they are?
- Is there any pattern or link with concerns raised in relation to role clarity, planning, evaluation, etc.?
- What does being organized mean to team members? What does it look like?
- What does being disorganized mean to team members? What does it look like?

Suggested approaches

Work with the team to review work processes, identifying which processes and interdependencies are critical to success. Where do they need to be changed? Depending on the nature and size of the team, this could take a couple of weeks. As part of this process, review how decisions are made in the team. Is the best expertise always available for specific decisions?

Does the work of the team need to be broken down into sub-groups charged with delivering specific aspects of the goals, or do current subgroups need to be realigned? Considering this element of alignment opens opportunities to examine ways to increase the empowerment of team members, including considering how team members can be given more responsibility.

In addition to ensuring the team delivers on agreed goals, leaders may have a specific responsibility to develop and grow future talent. This may mean planning to lose people and nurturing replacements and ensuring internal knowledge transfer between team members. This will ensure there is no drop in productivity when talent is promoted or moves on. Failure to develop people or allow talent to advance their career may result in frustrated team members staying but reducing their voluntary additional effort (their motivation, in other words). Alternatively, it may be the case that people leave the team and no replacements are ready to step into the breach. This can feel like a lack of control and management – a lack of organization.

This is a real issue today for any team leader and, whether it is an organizational requirement or not, it is good practice to have a strategy in place to address these issues. Millennials and the advent of giggers makes this scenario much more common and challenging.

A question of morale or motivation?

Morale is impacted by belief in the team leader and their ability to lead and organize the team in the most appropriate manner. To generate loyalty (that sense of wanting to belong) within the team, there must first and foremost be loyalty to the team leader. This loyalty is earned by demonstrating good leadership skills. Organization is one of them and this concept of organization permeates all other aspects of team effectiveness. No one wants to belong to a disorganized team. It is frustrating, and it undermines confidence, now and in the future. Why would someone want to work in such an environment? Remember that morale is experienced, and a poorly organized team is a poor experience for all. If your team's morale is poor, they will never exercise motivation – they cannot.

Key focus for the team leader: Have a discussion around 'how we are organized' with team members. They will have positive or negative views about what organization means to them and will share them if they are asked – but you have to ask them. In a team session, explore these views and what the team needs and wants in terms of organization.

Map the flow of work in a critical path. Look for overlaps, gaps and potentials for role and work duplication. Review all job roles and make sure that the full complement of relevant team members' skills are being used appropriately.

Consider issues such as the amount of overtime being worked. Question it – why is it necessary? Can it be reduced through better organization of resources and tasks? Or is it the case that there are insufficient resources in terms of people and/or equipment and the tools to do the job? If skills gaps are identified as an issue, develop a plan to close them.

In the coffee world, familiarizing yourself with the different types of roast and their characteristics is the only way to predict the flavour of the coffee beans to be brewed. The roast is responsible for determining the aroma, acidity, body and flavour of your chosen bean. Dark roasts, for example, do not produce a stronger cup but rather a more consistent one. The roast you choose will depend on the flavours or the feel of coffee you prefer, as well as what kind of coffee you are brewing.

Organization is about predicting and managing risk in terms of the goals to be achieved – building confidence for outcomes. Like coffee, where and how you roast determines what ends up in the cup, organization determines what can be managed and predicted.

Endnotes.

1 Wilson, David S. *Does Altruism Exist? Culture, Genes, and the Welfare of Others.* New Haven: Yale University Press, 2015.

2 Jeffery, Robert. "Who Needs Staff? The Decline of Full-Time Employment." *People Management,* 26 April 2017. Accessed 20 April 2018. https://www.peoplemanagement.co.uk/long-reads/articles/who-needs-staff.

3 Upwork. "New Study Finds Freelance Economy Grew to 55 Million Americans This Year, 35% of Total US Workforce." Accessed 18 February 2018. https://www.upwork.com/press/2016/10/06/freelancing-in-america-2016.

4 Deloitte. *Global Human Capital Trends 2015: Leading in the New World of Work.* Deloitte University Press, 2015.

5 Schawbel, Dan. "10 Ways Millennials Are Creating the Future of Work." Forbes, 16 December 2013. Accessed 18 February 2018. https://www.forbes.com/sites/danschawbel/2013/12/16/10-ways-millennials-are-creating-the-future-of-work/#1b08753c3105.

6 Deloitte. *Global Human Capital Trends 2016 – The New Organization: Different by Design.* Deloitte University Press, 2016. Accessed 18 February 2018. https://www2.deloitte.com/content/dam/Deloitte/global/Documents/HumanCapital/gx-dup-global-human-capital-trends-2016.pdf.

7 Deloitte. *Global Human Capital Trends 2017: Rewriting the Rules for a Digital Age.* Deloitte University Press, 2017. Accessed 18 February 2018. https://www2.deloitte.com/content/dam/Deloitte/global/Documents/About-Deloitte/central-europe/ce-global-human-capital-trends.pdf.

8 Shapiro, Eileen. *Fad Surfing in the Boardroom.* Reading: Addison-Wesley, 1995.

9 Bureau of Labor Statistics. "Labor Productivity and Costs." United States Department of Labor, 2018. Accessed 18 February 2018. https://www.bls.gov/lpc/prodybar.htm.

10 Belbin, R. Meredith. *Beyond the Team.* Oxford: Butterworth Heinemann, 2000.

11 Hackman, J.R. and N.J. Vidmar. "Effects of Size and Task Type on Group Performance and Member Reactions." *Sociometry,* no. 33 (1970): 37–54.

12 Dunbar, R. "Neocortex Size as a Constraint on Group Size in Primates." *Journal of Human Evolution*, vol. 22, no. 6 (1992): 469–493.

13 Wageman, Ruth, Debra A. Nunes, James A.J. Burruss and J. Richard Hackman. *Senior Leadership Teams: What It Takes to Make Them Great (Leadership for the Common Good)*. Boston: Harvard Business School, 2008.

14 Rozovsky, Julia. "The Five Keys to a Successful Google Team." Google, 17 November 2015. Accessed 18 February 2018. https://rework.withgoogle.com/blog/five-keys-to-a-successful-google-team.

15 Kahn, William A. "Psychological Conditions of Personal Engagement and Disengagement at Work." *Academy of Management Journal*, vol. 33, no. 4 (1990): 692–724.

16 Lewin, Kurt. *Resolving Social Conflicts: Selected Papers on Group Dynamics*, edited by Gertrude Weiss Lewin. New York: Harper and Brothers, 1948.

17 Edmondson, Amy. "Building a Psychologically Safe Workplace." YouTube, May 2014. Accessed 18 February 2018. https://www.youtube.com/watch?v=LhoLuui9gX8.

18 Jain, Anshu K., Mary L. Fennell, Anees B. Chagpar, Hannah K. Connolly and Ingrid M. Nembhard. "Moving Toward Improved Teamwork in Cancer Care: The Role of Psychological Safety in Team Communication." *Journal of Oncology Practice*, vol. 12, no. 11 (2016). Accessed 18 February 2018. http://ascopubs.org/doi/pdf/10.1200/JOP.2016.013300.

19 Schippers, Michaéla C., Michael A. West and Jeremy F. Dawson. "Team Reflexivity and Innovation: The Moderating Role of Team Context." *Journal of Management*, vol. 41, no. 3 (2015): 769–788.

20 Lykins, Lorrie. "2/3 of Companies Are Reengineering Performance Management." Institute for Corporate Productivity, 1 December 2016. Accessed 18 February 2018. https://www.i4cp.com/productivity-blog/2-3-of-companies-are-reengineering-performance-management.

21 Buckingham, Marcus and Ashley Goodall. "Reinventing Performance Management." *Harvard Business Review*, April 2015. Accessed 18 February 2018. https://hbr.org/2015/04/reinventing-performance-management.

22 Mayer, Joe. "Four Ways to Measure Team Performance: How a Team Functions Can Make or Break a Business." The Fabricator, 25 November 2013. Accessed 18 February 2018. https://www.thefabricator.com/article/shopmanagement/four-ways-to-measure-team-performance.

23 Society for Human Resource Management. *Global Diversity and Inclusion: Perceptions, Practices and Attitudes.* 2009. Accessed 18 February 2018. https://www.shrm.org/hr-today/trends-and-forecasting/research-and-surveys/Documents/09-Diversity_and_Inclusion_Report.pdf.

24 Krivkovich, Alexis, Kelsey Robinson, Irina Starikova, Rachel Valentino and Lareina Yee. "Women in the Workplace 2017." McKinsey & Company, October 2017. Accessed 18 February 2018. https://www.mckinsey.com/global-themes/gender-equality/women-in-the-workplace-2017.

25 Belbin. 2018. Accessed 18 February 2018. http://www.belbin.com.

26 Insights. 2018. Accessed 18 February 2018. https://www.insights.com.

27 Myers Briggs. 2018. Accessed 18 February 2018. http://www.myersbriggs.org.

28 Discprofile. 2018. Accessed 18 February 2018. https://discprofile.com.

29 True Colors Intl. 2018. Accessed 18 February 2018. https://truecolorsintl.com.

30 Wineinger Co. 2018. Accessed February 2018. https://thewineingercompany.com/about-birkman.

31 Hogan Assessments. 2018. Accessed 18 February 2018. https://www.hoganassessments.com.

32 CEB Global. 2018. Accessed 18 February 2018. https://www.cebglobal.com/talent-management/talent-assessment/assessments/shl-opq.html.

33 The ODD Company. 2018. Accessed 18 February 2018. http://www.theoddcompany.ie.

34 Wegner, Daniel, Paula Raymond and Ralph Erber. "Transactive Memory in Close Relationships." *Journal of Personality and Social Psychology*, vol. 61, no. 6 (1991): 923–929.

35 Lawrence, Paul R. and Jay W. Lorsch. "Differentiation and Integration in Complex Organizations." *Administrative Science Quarterly,* vol. 12, no. 1 (1967): 1–47.

36 Aston, Ben. "9 Project Management Methodologies Made Simple: The Complete Guide for Project Managers." The Digital Project Manager, 2 March 2017. Accessed 18 February 2018. https://thedigitalproject-manager.com/project-management-methodologies-made-simple.

37 Ferrazzi, Keith. "Getting Virtual Teams Right." *Harvard Business Review*, December 2014. Accessed 18 February 2018. https://hbr.org/2014/12/getting-virtual-teams-right.

38 Lojeski, Karen and Richard Reilly. *Uniting the Virtual Workforce:
Transforming Leadership and Innovation in the Globally Integrated
Enterprise.* Hoboken: John Wiley & Sons, 2008.

39 Edmondson, Amy C. *Teaming: How Organizations Learn,
Innovate, and Compete in the Knowledge Economy.*
San Francisco: Jossey-Bass, 2012.

40 Fournies, Ferdinand. *Coaching for Improved Work Performance.*
New York: McGraw-Hill, 2000.

41 McGregor, Douglas. *The Human Side of Enterprise, Annotated Edition.*
New York: McGraw-Hill, 2006.

42 Herzberg, Frederick. "One More Time: How Do You Motivate
Employees?" *Harvard Business Review*, September–October 1987.
Accessed 18 February 2018. https://pdfs.semanticscholar.org/ca2a/
a2ae02ac5b738b55b12b7324fac59571b1c1.pdf.

43 Latham, Gary P. and Edwin A. Locke. "Enhancing the Benefits and
Overcoming the Pitfalls of Goal Setting." *Organizational Dynamics*,
vol. 35, no. 4 (2006): 332–338.

44 Vroom, Victor. *Work and Motivation.*
New York: John Wiley & Sons, 1964.

45 Maslow, Abraham H. "A Theory of Human Motivation."
Psychological Review, vol. 50, no. 4 (1943): 370–396.

46 Thomas, Kenneth W. and Ralph H. Kilmann. "An Overview
of the Thomas-Kilmann Conflict Mode Instrument (TKI)."
Kilmann Diagnostics, August 2015. Accessed 18 February 2018.
http://www.kilmanndiagnostics.com/
overview-thomas-kilmann-conflict-mode-instrument-tki.

47 Lehman Brothers Centre for Women in Business. *Innovative Potential:
Men and Women in Teams.* London Business School, 2007.
Accessed 18 February 2018. https://www.lnds.net/blog/
images/2013/09/grattonreportinnovative_potential_nov_2007.pdf.

48 Chandler McCleod Group. "Collective Intelligence: Unleashing
Potential to Create High Performing Teams." Issuu, 22 July 2016.
Accessed 18 February 2018. https://issuu.com/chandlermacleodgroup/
docs/cm3086_05.16_cmpi_ci_ebook.

49 Hamm, John. "Why Entrepreneurs Don't Scale." *Harvard Business
Review*, December 2002. Accessed 18 February 2018.
https://hbr.org/2002/12/why-entrepreneurs-dont-scale.

About the author.

Simon Mac Rory is a specialist in team development. He works with senior staff leaders to help them discover that edge to becoming a truly high-performing team. Over his 30-year career he has worked globally with a blue-chip client base in both the private and public sectors.

He founded The ODD Company in 2011 to deliver TDP – a cloud-based team development tool and methodology – to the international markets. Simon operates the business from London with a Dublin-based development and support office.

Simon received his doctoral degree for his work on the application of generic frameworks in organizational development and is a Visiting Research Fellow at Nottingham Business School.

TH

LID
ANNIVERSARY

Sharing knowledge since 1993

- 1993 Madrid
- 2008 Mexico DF and Monterrey
- 2010 London
- 2011 New York and Buenos Aires
- 2012 Bogotá
- 2014 Shanghai